THE DISCOMFORT ZONE

How to Get What You Want by Living Fearlessly

FARRAH STORR

PIATKUS

PIATKUS

First published in Great Britain in 2018 by Piatkus
This paperback edition published in Great Britain in 2021 by Piatkus

1 3 5 7 9 10 8 6 4 2

A CIP catalogue record for this book
is available from the British Library.

ISBN 978-0-349-4153-76

Typeset in Garamond by M Rules
Printed and bound in Great Britain by Clays Ltd, Elcograf S.p.A.

Papers used by Piatkus are from well-managed forests
and other responsible sources.

Piatkus
An imprint of
Little, Brown Book Group
Carmelite House
50 Victoria Embankment
London EC4Y 0DZ

An Hachette UK Company
www.hachette.co.uk

www.littlebrown.co.uk

ABOUT THE AUTHOR

Farrah Storr is an award-winning journalist and editor-in-chief of *Elle* UK. She was the launch editor-in-chief of *Women's Health* in the UK, and was also editor-in-chief of *Cosmopolitan* UK. In 2017 she was named as one of the country's top five female BAME leaders in the UK by the *Guardian* and Operation Black Vote.

She lives in the country with her husband and two dogs. This is her first book.

To William, Parker and Jones

CONTENTS

PROLOGUE

Introducing the brief moments of discomfort (BMD) method

Have you ever had the sense of being stared at? I have – by twenty-five different pairs of eyes, all at once. It was my first day on the job as editor-in-chief of *Cosmopolitan* magazine and my new office was a glass box, twelve feet by twelve feet, slap bang in the middle of the office floor. It had one window that looked down on the streets of Soho below, an old navy-blue leather sofa in one corner (graciously left behind by the former beloved editor) and three glass walls that looked out over twenty-five desks, behind which sat my new team. Except on that summer morning in 2015, I wasn't quite sure they wanted me there. And the truth was, I wasn't quite sure I wanted to be there either.

Just a few weeks earlier I'd been editing a much smaller magazine in the same building. It had been my first editorship and the magazine, a health title called, rather unoriginally, *Women's Health*, was one I had grown to love. I had launched it three years earlier from an airless back room with just two members of staff and an almost non-existent budget. The hours were long, the pay was bad and we'd had just eight weeks in which to get an issue together from scratch. Oh ... and we had to sell 100,000 copies from issue one. And if we hadn't? Well, then the magazine would have folded along with all the other women's magazines toppling around us like dominoes – and we'd all have been out of jobs. I took the gamble regardless, after all, I figured, how hard could it be?

Three weeks into that job and hard didn't even cover it. Celebrities wouldn't speak to us ('Women's *what* ... ', their agents drawled down the phone); writers wouldn't write for us ('I've never heard of this magazine in my life ... sounds like a vitamin supplement') and even I was doubtful that we'd get it off the ground in time.

And yet, along the way, something miraculous happened. The obstacles that I'd worried would trip us up – lack of money, lack of people-power, lack of time – were the very things that made us soar. Our lack of resources forced us to be wildly inventive. We hustled with a ferociousness only the desperate can truly understand. (And to all those picture agencies, model agencies and celebrity agents out there – please forgive us our trespasses. We literally knew not what we did.) We were irreverent and bold in a way only the stupid or the damned can be. We experimented with new writers, new photographers, and came up with inventive (read cheap) ways to illustrate our stories, because the truth was we couldn't afford to be conventional. Convention was expensive.

We held our breath when the first issue went on sale on 4 January 2012. Within twenty-four hours the sales figures started to trickle in. Then the emails. Then the congratulatory messages from advertisers who loved the product. It was exciting! It was naughty! It was funny in a way that health magazines had never been before! By the end of the month we had sold 103,000 copies. That number went up and up as the months went by. Awards started to gather. By the end of the year, we were, to our absolute disbelief, hailed as the 'most successful women's magazine launch of the decade'.

By the summer of 2015 I had been editing *Women's Health* for exactly three years and eight months. We had grown into a team of twelve who were as tight and close to a work family as I had ever known. I knew my colleagues' families and they knew mine. One of them even drove me 200 miles to pick up my puppy during the coldest, snowiest winter to hit Britain in twenty-five years. Things finally felt . . . comfortable.

And then I got the call to go and edit *Cosmopolitan*.

Now, if this were a film, this is the point at which this scene would pause while I give you some qualifying backstory as to why this was not the idyllic scenario it at first appears. *Cosmo* was struggling. Its readership numbers were dwindling. I opened the magazine and found very little had changed since first reading it twenty years earlier. There were still agony aunts in it – the same one, in fact, that I had been taking advice from about what to do with a flaccid penis back in 1990. There were still articles on ten ways to give blow jobs (seriously – was anyone even giving them in 2015?) and a deeply uncomfortable-looking naked male centrefold, who turned out to be some guy who came fifth in *The Apprentice*. It was still a great magazine, no doubt, but it also needed turning around, and quickly. The thing was, I didn't know if I was the person who could do that. Firstly, I would be replacing one of the best and most adored editors in the business – a woman who I'd looked up to my entire career, but one I knew the team loved like their own mothers. To make a real change I'd also need to do something radical, and to do that I'd get people's backs up from day one – everyone from the team to the hundreds of thousands of loyal *Cosmo* readers across the globe. *Cosmopolitan* was the biggest female media brand in the world. I didn't want to be the one who dug its grave.

And yet, forty-eight hours later I decided to take the job. Why? Because I needed to be pushed. I needed to feel the same frisson of nerves and tension that had characterised my first few months at *Women's Health*. I needed to be pushed into my discomfort zone.

And so there I was, on my first official day in the office, alone, in my glass cube. Only a few boxes had arrived from my previous office, the rest somehow lost in transit along with, inexplicably, my desk. The only thing that had made the short journey from my old office at *Women's Health* to my new office at *Cosmo* was an enormous, comedic, stand-up desk . . . and I was wearing six-inch heels.

I stood behind it, my feet sore, my back aching, and looked out. I felt ridiculous – ridiculous and scared out of my mind. You see, my brain did not see the twenty-five members of the *Cosmopolitan* team outside my door as individuals, but rather as one giant, hostile mass. Every one of them, my brain told me, didn't want me there. Every one of them wanted me to fail.

But it's a funny thing, the human brain. It lies. It looks for easy absolutes to create a scary narrative. A narrative that, if you're not careful, will paralyse you. I had discovered this a few weeks previously, when taking a short break before joining the magazine. The hotel I was staying at had an outdoor pool. It was a beautiful emerald-green thing, as still and pretty as a Monet lily pond, and every morning I vowed to swim in it. There was just one issue: it was freezing. Properly bone-rattlingly cold. Still, every morning I would rise at the crack of dawn, head down despite being bleary with sleep, slip off my robe and get as far as the edge of the pool. I would then dip my forefinger in with all the slow deliberation of Nigella Lawson lowering her index finger into a bowl of butter cream, retract it and then head back to the hotel. By day three I had not completed a single lap.

The problem, I realised, was that my brain was viewing the pool as one giant ice block, registering it as one long, continuous struggle. Of course, I knew that wasn't true – after all, there were about five other people in there every morning. Sure, there would be a moment of internal struggle as I decided whether to change into my swimming costume. Then there would be a small amount of discomfort as I first stepped into the pool. And then it would be crunch time – the nasty moment of true discomfort when I had to submerge my entire body in the water. But once that was done? That would be it.

On my final day I went to my suitcase, pulled my swimsuit on without even thinking, and walked purposefully down to the pool. I sat on the edge, and dipped my foot in. It was arctic. Still, I gritted my teeth and slid in until half of my body was submerged. That was the horrid part, the 'crunch point', hanging there, suspended between the searing cold water that encased my legs and hips while the rest of my body was open to the warm sun. Ordinarily I would stand like that for some minutes, *struggling*. I would prolong the pain as my brain flitted between two courses of action: easy way *out* or hard way *in*.

But here's the thing: the idea that leaving the pool was an 'easy way out' was not strictly true. It was a trick conjured up by my brain. Leaving the pool at that 'crunch point' would have been just as uncomfortable as ploughing my entire body under the water. It would have involved pulling myself out of the pool, exposing my wet body to the air, while, let's not forget, embarrassing myself in front of my audience of four floating pensioners. The 'hard way in', on the other hand, meant a *brief* moment of shock as my body was swallowed up by the freezing water. And so that's what I did. I counted to three, held my breath and descended into the discomfort.

I don't remember the exact length of time it took before my teeth stopped chattering, but it would have been mere seconds. The pain was intense, yes, but fleeting. So quick, in fact, that I barely remembered it once I started to swim. Instead, I only remember the sun on the surface of the water, the waiter who placed a drink by my sun lounger and the fact that I felt relaxed and triumphant for the first time in months.

And so, on that first morning at *Cosmopolitan*, I thought back to that brief moment of discomfort in the pool. Armed with that knowledge, I told myself that there would be only short periods of pain. The entire day, week, month would not, as I had initially thought, be one long, drawn-out drama. Of course, there would be discomfort as I told the office my radical plans for the magazine, but it would only last those few seconds as everyone clamoured in my office, not for the entire conversation. And sure, there would be some discomfort when I told certain members of the team that their work would need some tinkering, but the pain would only last the few minutes it took me to explain.

Without exception, discomfort is never as bad as we think it will be. It also never lasts as long as we think it will. Because here is what I have learned: discomfort is not a constant; it is fleeting. Neither is discomfort debilitating; on the contrary, it is *empowering*. However, it has taken me years to realise this, years of being thrown into deeply uncomfortable situations time and again – often through no choice of my own – in order to figure this out. I have moved to the other side of the world for a disastrous job (more of which later); have inadvertently found myself on a stage in front of 20,000 people, completely unprepared as to what to say (the stuff of genuine nightmares) and been moments away from being sacked from my first job in journalism. But had I not unwillingly found myself in these difficult situations, I would not *willingly* throw myself into similar scenarios in the manner in which I do today. Because facing true discomfort not only helped unlock who I was, but, more crucially, helped unlock who and what I had the capacity to become.

Getting comfortable with being uncomfortable is the mantra I now subscribe to. And you will too, once you realise how doing so has the power to unleash your true potential. (Remember when you were growing up and your parents were always crowing on about how you weren't 'reaching your full potential', and you were like: 'What is this *thing* called potential? And how do I know when I've reached it? Well, stepping into your discomfort zone is the quickest way to find it.)

And by the way … if this all sounds like hard work for life's most hardened masochists, full disclosure time: I'm not tougher than your average woman. I've also not benefitted from any extraordinary childhood that would prepare me more for living this sort of life than you. In fact, I'm not tough at all. I was the kid who screamed at the nursery-school gates when her mother kissed her goodbye. I'm the person who could (if allowed) spend all night locked in the toilet cubicle at a public function. I'm the person who, when asked to give a few impromptu 'words' in front of a crowd, feels as though her sphincter muscle is about to give way. Or at least I *was* that person, before I got comfortable with the uncomfortable. Now? I can breeze through all of it without having a cardiac arrest midway. Better than that, I *enjoy* these situations. And you have my absolute word: once you discover the ease with which anyone can appreciate discomfort, you will too.

THE BMD METHOD

Momentary. That's what all pain and discomfort is. You know those little wax strips that you pat onto your moustache and rogue chin hairs? (Men, close your ears and shut down all visual imagery *now* please.) That's what discomfort is: teeny, tiny little frissons of pain that pass almost instantaneously. When you give a public speech, the only bit that's really uncomfortable is the part just before you walk on stage. Okay, or maybe the first three seconds as you look out at all those faces staring back at you. But after that? It's fine. You're in motion. You don't have time to register pain or difficulty. Your brain is too busy working on the situation in hand.

I'll give you another example. You know when a well-meaning colleague comes round with cake and you're thirty minutes into some bizarre newfangled deprivation diet? Well, your 'crunch point' (and by that I'm referring to the most uncomfortable point in your teeny, tiny moment of discomfort) is that second when your mouth is salivating, the cake is in your direct eyeline and you must either shake or nod your head to confirm or deny access. Once you've made that decision, and the cake has left the premises, it's easy. Your brain moves on to something else.

I call these BMDs – Brief Moments of Discomfort. Anyone, and I mean *anyone*, can charge through short periods of change and pain. After all, most of us already do it every single day of our lives. We just don't *willingly* do it. I bet you've already had several BMDs today. Saying no to another drink after work, say (even though you desperately want one), or having a confrontation with the difficult receptionist at your gym – these are all BMDs. The difference is, they were imposed on you, rather than you imposing them on yourself. What's the difference? Well, the difference is *huge*. When uncomfortable situations are thrust upon us we have no control. And not having control can lead to alarming consequences. But uncomfortable situations that you have imposed upon yourself give you the opportunity to go into them with a plan. And having a roadmap when you find you've drifted far out of your comfort zone and in to the choppy waters of your discomfort zone is what leads to magical outcomes.

The BMD method is something I have been using for the past five years of my life. And since following it, not only have I transformed the way I live my life, but also the quality of the life I live. I take more risks, because I am no longer paralysed with fear about the outcome of those risks. And by taking those seemingly 'uncomfortable' risks, new unthinkable opportunities have opened up for me. I'll give you an example: a big part of my job is now public speaking across the world, something I would *never* have believed could be an option for me. And it wouldn't have, unless I had put myself into my discomfort zone to begin with.

So what is the BMD method? And how will it change your life? It's simple. The BMD method is a formula that *anyone* can use for *any* seemingly difficult situation. It's not complex and it doesn't take time to remember. It's nothing more than a three-point plan that you can use during any time or situation where you feel out of your 'comfort zone'. You can use the BMD method for life, although the more I use it, the less I need it. That's because once you start to use it you will, as if by magic, get stronger, more confident and feel more in control of your life. I know, I know, these sound like big, lofty promises that a man on a stage with a head mic and his hands pressed together in 'pyramid pose' might throw at you. But this is real. I promise.

Step one: Acknowledge your fear

In many ways this is the hardest bit, because it requires a smidgen of honesty on your part. This is the part where you stop pretending that you can 'conquer the world' (because if you can, how come you haven't already?) and acknowledge what scares you. It involves *you* identifying where your comfort zone ends and your discomfort zone begins. This is crucial, because simply finding yourself in, or indeed being thrown into, your discomfort zone can be hugely traumatic. You feel out of control, so you make quick, often erroneous and *risky* decisions. And if you're traumatised then you're unlikely to ever repeat the experience again. (Though, as you will also see from Chapter Three, there can be some positive outcomes from traumatic situations. But we'll get on to that.) Through the BMD method you will not only be able to identity the *exact* moment in which you step into your discomfort zone, but you will also understand all the associated feelings you experience when you're there (racing heart, sweaty palms, undulating intestinal movement . . . yeah, *I know*). But it's absolutely crucial that you identify, acknowledge and understand these physiological reactions because that's the first step in helping you control them.

Step two: Identify your moments of discomfort

If step one was about helping you to move into your discomfort zone, then step two is about making you feel (ironically enough) *comfortable* once you're there. There are two types of comfort. First there is 'deadly comfort'. Deadly comfort is the sort that has people rotting in dead-end jobs and comatose relationships. Deadly comfort is like those animal onesies we all thought were a good idea to wear sloping around the house in 2012, until we found our bodies, beneath all that synthetic animal fur, were starting to resemble said animal. (I gained an entire dress size – that's what deadly comfort does for you.) Deadly comfort requires zero thought, zero discipline and will ultimately give you zero gains.

'Active comfort', however, is a whole different ballgame. This is a positive state of being, rather than a lazy state of mind. 'Active comfort' means feeling comfortable in an uncomfortable situation – and who wouldn't want that? The BMD method will teach you how to identify the three main, brief moments of discomfort in any situation (it's unusual for there to be more than this – again, I'll explain later) and solutions on how to get through them. These solutions are your 'BMD arsenal' and can be anything from having a four-second silence before you start a speech in order to get people's attention (works like a dream) to having a line prepared should you not be able to answer a question in a job interview. (Me? I always say: 'I can't answer that for you at the minute, but I can give you <insert diversionary piece of information here so you are at least saying *something*>.') Having a BMD arsenal is key to making you feel comfortable in any unknowable situation.

Step three: Reimagining discomfort

This is the fun bit where you start imagining all the things you could do with your life because you have sussed out what discomfort actually is. Essentially, in step three you recognise that discomfort is little more than a few nanoseconds of feeling uncomfortable. You start to see that discomfort is not disruptive but constructive. You begin to understand that it is not oppressive but uplifting and you see, *finally*, through the clearing mist, that discomfort is not about difficult struggle but about invigorating challenge.

Basically, what you will find by adopting the BMD method is that nothing in life is an insurmountable challenge, but rather a series of small, uncomfortable tests that can easily be overcome. The most difficult situations are not, as our brains lead us to believe, huge, terrifying experiences, but brief moments of pain that pass within seconds. I like to think of them as high-intensity interval training for your life. Once you understand the bite-sized nature of your fear you'll be able to take on anything. In time, you'll even begin to enjoy these moments.

This is now how I approach everything in my life – big speeches I'm asked to give, confrontations I have to endure, parties I have to attend where I won't know a single person. Understanding that everything I fear can be broken down into three simple 'crunch points' has allowed me to take on challenges I would ordinarily side-step. Or approach with stomach-churning dread. You can't escape discomfort. In fact, those very situations where we feel alarmingly out of our depth are crucial for progression and success. But if you understand the secret of how to break through them, you can take on challenges you never thought possible – and achieve astonishing success along the way.

THE 'MIRACLE' OF STRESS

In 2008 the world felt like it was falling to pieces. Lehman Brothers, one of the world's largest global banks, had just filed for bankruptcy. A few months later, one of the US's largest insurance companies, AIG, did the same. The financial world was unravelling at its seams and taking with it the world's jobs, homes and minds.

We turned on the news and footage alternated between images of blank-eyed bankers being hounded out of their offices for crimes many of us did not yet quite understand (the whole subprime mortgage, CDO catastrophe is still difficult to get your head around) and American families being evicted from their homes. I will personally never forget seeing an entire family, complete with three dogs and twice as many children, vacating their large Spanish-style villa in Florida and then pointing to the family station wagon, explaining this was now home for the foreseeable future.

Of course, we now know that 2008 was the height of what has become known as the Financial Crisis – the most devastating global recession to hit the world since the Great Depression of the 1930s. At the time, however, few of us understood quite how serious the ramifications of dirty dealings by banks and bankers were – apart from the bankers themselves. This is perhaps why Dr Alia Crum, an assistant professor of psychology at Stanford University, and Shawn Achor, a positive psychologist and author of the excellent *The Happiness Advantage*, paid a visit to UBS bank to undertake a study on the effects of stress.

In 2008 the Swiss bank was not in a good way. Not only was there massive restructuring going on across the company, but the FBI had just begun a large-scale investigation into an alleged tax-evasion scheme. This was on top of the fact that banks were collapsing around them like sandcastles in the tide.

One can only imagine, then, that UBS bankers were less than thrilled to be the subjects of Crum and Achor's 'stress test'. Taking a sample of four hundred bankers, Crum and Achor split the largely male participants into three groups. The first group was taken into a room and made to watch a video that depicted stress as toxic and corrosive, a danger to both health and well-being. The second group, meanwhile, was shown a video with a very different angle: stress was depicted as a performance enhancer. (The third group was not forced to watch any clip and probably wondered what the hell was going on.)

A week later the three groups were reassembled. Each was then asked to report on how they had felt and performed at work after having watched the video clips. The group who had watched the toxic video on stress and the group who had watched no video at all reported no changes. However, the group who had sat through the clip depicting stress as a performance enhancer reported the following: greater focus and higher engagement at work, as well as fewer health problems than before.

Other experiments have demonstrated similar findings. A famous study on rats has shown that when these poor rodents are put under short periods of uncomfortable stress (in this case, being confined to small cages for short periods of time) their brain cells were shown to enlarge temporarily. Meanwhile, in his tremendous book *Bounce*, Matthew Syed found that it's not only the human mind but also the human body that responds positively to controlled amounts of discomfort.

Ultra-marathon runners, who have endured years of gruelling, often deeply uncomfortable ultra runs, have enlarged hearts as a result. Professional dancers, who must contort their bodies into the most agonising forms and shapes over years of practice, are rewarded with almost superhuman physiological abilities: feet that can turn at extraordinary angles, which surely all superheroes could do with. Professional pianists, similarly, have fingers that can flex and move far beyond the capabilities of mere mortals, a result of hours of challenging practice. (Interestingly, the part of their brains responsible for all that finger contortion is also shown to be significantly larger than your average Joe's.) There is even some thinking to suggest that Brazil consistently produces the world's best football players (Pelé, Ronaldinho, Ronaldo, Garrincha – the list goes on and on) due to the fact that young Brazilians learn to play football not with a light leather football on a soft, grass pitch as we do across much of the world, but by playing *futsal*.

Futsal is *difficult*. It is *uncomfortable*, especially when played with bare feet, as most young Brazilian kids do. It is also a fast-paced game played on a hard surface, with a smaller goal area, and with a ball that is firmer, heavier and has 30 per cent less bounce than your average football. That means the game requires more dexterity, greater creativity and greater skill at shooting. In other words, every time a child agrees to play a game of *futsal* they are throwing their bodies and minds into the discomfort zone. The result? Brazil has won more World Cup titles than any other country on earth.

So, you see, discomfort, and its associated stress, is not always the enemy we have been led to believe it is. If harnessed correctly, it can have enormous advantages and effects. From pro athletes to young kids on a dusty *futsal* pitch, a certain degree of stress is the difference between excellent and *exceptional*.

Of course, that's an unpopular view to espouse. (And, as the former editor of a health magazine, I'm sure you can imagine how well this idea goes down.) We live in an era of 'stress'. *Everyone* is stressed. Ask anyone how their week was and the ensuing answer is likely to produce the word stress at some point. Studies tell us that young people are more stressed than older people; women are more stressed than men; and if you live in the UK and are a young woman aged between eighteen and twenty-four you're the most stressed out of all right now.

But what if we have been treating the discomfort of stress all wrong? We have, after all, built an entire industry around protecting ourselves from it, rather than facing it head on. Over the last twenty-five years we have institutionalised stress, pathologised it, packaged it up and put a blue ribbon round it, then sold it back to ourselves as luxury retreats with zero Wi-Fi, and massages with stress-relieving juju powers. Every challenge we face, every obstacle that stands in our way, we slap a diagnostic label on – and that label is: stress.

And what has happened is this: we have become terrified of stress. It is toxic. It will massacre your brain cells. It will lacerate your immune system. It will make your heart beat like a tribesman's drum and pickle your internal organs in cortisol. Your blood pressure will be dizzyingly high, your hair will thin (and grey). Stress will pin its thumb down on your body and mind, leaving you wizened and cracked like a piece of gum on the pavement.

And yet we have created a culture in which we insulate ourselves from anything we perceive as harmful or stress-inducing. It's the reason why schools are still dishing out medals for first, second and . . . last. It's the same reason that children's homework is no longer marked in malignant red pen, but in pink, because red pen is seen as too 'damaging' and too indicative of failure.

In our universities we have seen the dawn of these strange new places known only as 'safe spaces': a coddled zone, free from noxious talk, dissenting viewpoints and basically any-thing that doesn't concur with our world view. There has been a boom in 'stress-relieving' colouring books for adults, while employers such as Nike and Uber now offer employees 'nap time' to help ease office tensions.

If that's not enough to eviscerate your stress woes then perhaps the Googlefication of offices across the land can help, where managers have substituted cold, corporate desks for 'chilled-out' bean-bag zones, evicted 'scary' meeting room tables in favour of ping pong ones, and ditched perfectly good internal staircases for 'giant slides' so that stressed-out grown men in polyester suits can come tumbling down like massive toddlers with canines.

Oh, and if work can't help you eradicate all that nasty stress then the lifestyle holiday sector can certainly help. Simply let them whizz you up a 'stress-free' break on which phones are taken from you like toys sequestered from naughty children, and extra-curricular activities include 'tug of war', 'apple bobbing' and evening 'singalongs'. (This is certifiably true and can be found along the east coast of America, servicing frazzled New Yorkers.)

But what if we have got it all wrong? What if a little bit of the right sort of stress is what we need? Because here is the thing: the human body is made to *strive*. It can, in fact, perform better under certain stressful conditions. It can not only survive discomfort but soar within its confines.

Remember, back when we were all doodling in caves, throwing woolly mammoth steaks on the barbecue and wearing bones like a Tiffany pendant, we were also on high alert most of the time. This was the environment in which we and our ancestors, and our ancestors before that, developed. Life was hard. Discomfort was the norm. We were hunter-gatherers, living in a world where we regularly experienced food shortages, swings in temperature and attack from animals five times our size. We had to tough it out to find food, and strive to keep warm and out of harm's way. We lived like this for thousands of years and, as such, evolution has paid us back by creating a human mind and body primed to experience daily stress and discomfort.

But modern life has slowly taken away these stressors. We call this progress. In the Western world there are now restaurants open twenty-four hours a day. You can buy your meals prechopped, precooked and predigested (seriously – it exists) and then get them delivered to your front door with a click of your computer. We have air con for when it's too hot and central heating for when it's too cold. Small, benign-looking robots (Google's Echo, Amazon's Alexa, Apple's HomePod) now share our homes. They sit on our kitchen counters and bedside tables waiting to be shouted at. 'ALEXA, change the radio station.' 'OK Google, how many grams of sugar do I need to make a lemon meringue pie?' I am waiting for the day someone brings out an AI machine that can empty your bladder for you. Here's hoping . . .

The point is, progress has limited us as much as it has advanced us. We have become so smart at reducing stress that it is literally killing us. We are now faced with some of the greatest health challenges of our time: obesity, diabetes, hypertension and inflammation – all of them by-products of insulating ourselves from the sort of stress our bodies and minds were designed to withstand. This book is a call for something some of you may find challenging to accept: that we need to embrace discomfort, not shield ourselves from it. We need to make it part of our everyday lives. We need to throw ourselves into it in order to stretch and test our capabilities. We need it in order to feel truly alive.

Successful people know and understand this. Show me a successful person who said the ride to success meant never stepping outside their 'comfort zone' and I'll show you someone who isn't quite as successful as they think they are. Our most revered leaders, athletes and politicians spend much of their lives living within their discomfort zone. Stephen King, Oprah Winfrey, J.K. Rowling, Jay-Z – these are all people whose true success began when they were forced into uncomfortable situations. (Oprah was fired from her first job, King's and J.K. Rowling's work was rejected multiple times at the beginning of their careers, while former drug dealer Jay-Z had to start his own record label after no one else would take him on.) It was a brush with discomfort that led each one of them to recognise the magical, life-enhancing alchemy that happened as a result. 'You learn more in failure than you ever do in success,' Jay-Z has since said. And amen to that.

In this book I have spoken to leaders, gold medal-winning athletes and regular men and women who excel at life. Their skills are great, sure, but their true secret is how they approach discomfort. Everyone, from the twenty-six-year-old dropout who changed the way the modern world dates to the award-winning female firefighter who has saved dozens of lives, will tell you how they step into their discomfort zone day in, day out – and of the remarkable results that have followed. Taking on board their lessons, as well as adopting the BMD method, will not only result in helping *you* make better decisions and braver choices, but will ultimately bring greater meaning and happiness to your life. Learning how to step into your discomfort zone *and* feel comfortable is the revolution you have been waiting for. You just didn't know it.

1

REFRAMING DISCOMFORT

Getting comfortable with the uncomfortable

How comfortable do you feel when adrenaline strikes? Are you ready for it, like an athlete on the starting line? Or do you shrink away, lock yourself in a toilet until the moment passes and then vow you'll never come face to face with it again? Or maybe, just maybe, you are the sort of person who is so catatonically afraid of that heart-throbbing, stomach-clenching feeling that you try and avoid *all* situations in which you know it will hit.

Growing up I was a sprinter. I had legs that spun like a Catherine wheel and could outrun any boy in class. I won every sports cup going, and on Tuesday and Thursday evenings would drag my poor, overworked mother down to the local athletics track to watch me practice. Practice was a breeze. Out there on the track, crouched on the starting line like a squirrel, I had no expectations other than that I would beat my last documented time (I could do 100 metres in 14.2 seconds – not bad for a twelve-year-old who still hadn't figured out how to change the loo roll back home.) I was in my element. I had what my coach called 'potential' – lots and *lots* of potential.

There were whispers of my being good enough to run for my county. And after that? Who knew? Maybe even trying out for the national team. I would lie awake in bed at night and imagine myself, resplendent in red, white and blue Lycra on the winner's podium, cradling my gold medal before shuffling off to be interviewed by Brendan Foster. There was just one problem: I couldn't perform at competition level.

The 'issues' would start the night before with a dry throat and a stomach that felt like Mike Tyson's fist was clenched around it. By the morning of the competition I was at my worst. I would get up, feel faint and then look in the mirror to see I was the colour of a spirulina smoothie. By the time we arrived at the running track and I'd seen the crowds and the other kids warming up, their legs swinging back and forth in dynamic stretches, I was a goner. I would wobble towards the starting line with every cell in my body trembling, wishing and praying it would all be over. And it soon was. The gun would pop and fifteen seconds later I'd dip over the finish line in fourth or fifth place, posting some of the slowest times I'd ever run. I'd throw on my jacket, walk towards the out-stretched arms of my mother and then slink into the back seat of the car. Mum would put Simply Red on the stereo while I crouched in the back, head down, trying to stifle big, dramatic sobs with my shell suit jacket to the strangulated warbles of Mick Hucknall. At thirteen, the very moment I should have been on the cusp of greatness, I quit running altogether.

The problem was that I was completely and utterly

overwhelmed by discomfort. I couldn't comprehend what was happening to me when adrenaline started to kick in. And certainly no one had prepared me for when it did. I saw my scratchy throat, persistent stomach knots and my 'starting-line shakes' as a sign that I wasn't ready to perform. That I couldn't hack it. I just wasn't made from the right 'stuff'. I had heard adults mention something about getting 'nerves' before a big race, but no one had thought to tell me how that would feel. No one had taken the time to explain that 'nerves' could be a good thing. No one knew, I don't suppose (this was the late eighties, remember, the decade in which no one knew sunbathing in cooking oil was a bad thing either), that adrenaline was not a sign to stop, but a sign to go on. Adrenaline, and the ensuing discomfort, was my body's way of getting ready for action. But kneeling there on the starting line, my legs rattling like a tambourine, I had passed the moment of 'peak adrenaline'. My body, rather than harnessing the power of discomfort, had caved in. And at that point it was all over.

In this chapter I am going to tell you how to get comfortable with discomfort. I am going to show you that all those feelings you thought were a sign you weren't ready for that big presentation – that big job interview, that presentation to your boss – are a sign that you are. I am going to make sure that pretty soon you'll be able to sit with those feelings of discomfort in the same way you'd sit at the end of a bar with a stirred Martini. Because if you are the sort of person who wants to stretch yourself, the sort of person who wants to feel about and test what you are made of, then you *have* to get comfortable with it – certainly if you want to push through and explore your true potential. We're always being told that the biggest rewards in life come from the greatest risks. But in order to take those risks, you need to accept that they come with some uncomfortable feelings. They will jangle you. They will make you question whether you're tough enough to face whatever it is you're going through. But they are the exact feelings that, if understood and computed in the right way, will be your greatest ally. Because all they are is adrenaline. Once you know and understand this, you've taken your first step to being able to deal with it. *Everyone* from heavyweight politicians to pro athletes goes through this. Everyone goes through the hair-raising, spine-tingling sensations of a pure adrenaline rush. The difference is, these people understand that without it they wouldn't be able to make the great breakthroughs that have defined their lives. And until you do, you won't either.

DISCOMFORT PARALYSIS

By now you'll know what adrenaline is and when it strikes. It's a natural feeling, built into human nature to help us thrive in difficult situations. It's what makes us run away when we hear loud, uncomfortable noises. You know, like the screech of peripheral family turning up outside your house at Christmas (didn't they get the memo about *never* being welcome after Uncle Andy fell into that four-hour wormhole talking about his redundancy and the boss you all suspected he would in fact murder before New Year?) – that, or the Footlocker sale starting. The problem is it's not the best feeling in the world.

Some people complain of dizziness. Others feel sick. Me? I need the toilet. Non-stop.

But for some people it debilitates them altogether. They can't move. They freeze. Their heads are like slot machines emptying of all sense and information. It's the moment when an adrenaline rush tips over into a panic attack. And the window in which this can happen is very small and *very* subtle. It can strike anyone, at any time. And when it's happened once, the likelihood of it happening again is high.

Some people call this stage fright. I call it 'discomfort paralysis'. Because that's what it is – a paralysis. A moment of such intense frustration and sensory breakdown that it can scar people for years. Sometimes forever.

An example: Daniel Day-Lewis, arguably one of the most fêted actors of his generation; a three-time Oscar winner; a man who is so stupidly talented that he can renounce acting altogether, run off to retrain as a Florentine cobbler (true story) and then come back and win the Best Actor Oscar for his role in *In Cold Blood*. But in 1989 he was performing as Hamlet on stage at the London National Theatre when, halfway through the production, he froze, walked off the stage and never returned. And that's no understatement. He found the act of performing in front of a live audience so overwhelming that he has never done theatre since. He calls the aftermath of that night so 'dreadful' that he upped sticks and moved to rural Ireland. He had suffered from 'discomfort paralysis'.

Actor Stephen Fry went one step further to avoid the excruciating pain of performing in a play in front of an audience, leaving the UK *entirely* so as not to suffer from 'discomfort paralysis'. (He has since, rather eloquently, described stage fright as akin to the audience seeing 'the shrivelled penis inside your head'.) Actor Laurence Olivier suffered from intermittent bouts throughout his fifties. (It can strike at any point in your life, by the way, so even if you're okay with it now, there's no guarantee that's going to last. Sorry.) Grammy award-winning singer-songwriter Carly Simon took six years off from live performing because she became so overwhelmed and uncomfortable. The list of those who, at one point in their career suffered from 'discomfort paralysis' is as long as it is varied: Gandhi, Thomas Jefferson, one of the world's richest men Warren Buffett, opera singer Renée Fleming, actress Bette Midler, singer Adele. And yet each one has gone on to become a leading light in their professional field. So, what is their secret? To understand that, you first have to understand why they freaked out in the first place.

Let's say you're about to give a talk. Maybe you've been chosen to give a short speech at a friend's wedding. Or the boss has asked you to deliver a few well-wishing words to a departing colleague from your team. Simple enough requests. There is, on the surface, no imminent sense of danger. So why, then, do you feel sick? Why do you feel the 'freeze' coursing through your body at the very moment you're about to speak?

As I've mentioned before, your body, when put under stress, goes into flight or fight mode. Most of us recognise why this is: you either need to hightail the hell out of there when things get scary (flight), or you need to stick around and put up a fight. But there's a third response that doesn't get nearly as much attention and which we have almost all felt: *freezing*.

Freezing and 'discomfort paralysis' go hand in hand. It's that incapacitating feeling when everything – thoughts, feelings, normal human utterances – are catapulted out of the window. You are left rooted to the spot, unable to even make single eye twitches or small guttural sounds. It seems like an eternity (it rarely is – a few seconds at most) but it can derail everything. You have probably seen a performer suffer from discomfort paralysis on stage. Their eyes enlarge, their mouth hangs open and they stand straight and rigid as a meerkat. It's as painful to watch as it is to endure. And it's the fastest route to losing the confidence of everyone who witnesses it.

Here's the abridged version of what happens: that moment before you decided to fight or flee you freeze for a few milliseconds to assess the situation before making your next move. Your eyes open a little wider as you take in all the information around you, your mouth opens as you prepare to scream or shout, and you stand there, seemingly unable to move as you conserve energy for your next action.

This all sounds perfectly sensible, a smart evolutionary response to a fearful situation. But sometimes those milliseconds extend into seconds, then a few more seconds, and, before you know it, you're stranded, stuck in 'discomfort paralysis' from which it is very difficult to return.

Why does this happen? Well, it's thought that, without any real imminent danger in modern life (no wild cats or cave bears batting down our mud huts) we instead started to obsess about outcomes and fret about things we *think* might be dangerous. We forecast fear, so to speak, and in doing that we essentially juice up our amygdala, the bit of our brain that deals with fear and anticipation. And that's when the trouble starts. Is there a way to short-circuit this response? Is it even within our conscious power to escape from discomfort paralysis? And if so, how quickly can we make it work for us?

Most of us have taken exams at some point in our lives. I grew up at a time when exams meant *everything*. It didn't matter if you had performed well all year – if you didn't get the grade at exam time, then you were done. It was over. The academic group you would be in, which college you would go to and the university you would set sail for were all determined by how well you performed under examination conditions. And that was tough. While the curriculum and methods for testing students have changed since my day, exams are still part of everyone's education. And I tend to think that's right. In life you're always going to come up against stressful, deeply uncomfortable situations where you have only a short amount of time in which to impress. Getting a handle on how you do this at as early an age as possible is crucial.

The best place to see the acutely different reactions to adrenaline are outside an exam hall. You will notice the different poses. Some students will be hunched, taking deep gulps of air while looking skywards in a sort of trembling supplication to the exam gods. Others, meanwhile, will have chests puffed, arms stretched and hips thrust forward as though about to charge into coital battle. Make no mistake, both sets of students are in the grip of adrenaline. It's just that the grip is slightly different for each. The first set – the ones who look as though they are about to face the guillotine – are perceiving the exam as a threat, and in this state a whole series of dreadful outcomes are running through their minds: What if I fail? What if

I don't have enough time to complete everything? What if I get a question on the one thing I didn't prep for? (Sound familiar? That was me for pretty much all my student life.) The other set of students, however, see the exam as a challenge. They feel 'pumped', scared, yes, but also motivated to get on with the whole thing. They are in the grip of what researchers call a 'challenge state': the hormones that activate the brain's reward centre suppress fear. Seriously, they actively dampen it down. This means you are excited and invigorated, as opposed to feeling as though you're about to expurgate your entire insides. And here's what else happens: your blood vessels dilate, along with your lungs, which means you're getting more oxygen into your bloodstream. That means you can make sharper decisions, in less time. In other words, you are on metaphorical fire, primed to tackle whatever challenge is in front of you.

Now I know what you're thinking: but this is genetic, surely? Some people are able to see stressful situations as a challenge while others, okay, most of us, crumble. Of course, there are some out there who are genetically predisposed to react well under stressful conditions. As for the rest of us, we can learn it. We can actually learn how to prime ourselves better for those adrenaline-fuelled situations. Here's how. Interested? I thought that might be the case . . .

SMARTER SELF-TALK

When people say, 'I'm stressed out', it basically means 'I'm not doing great'. It doesn't mean, 'I'm excited – I have increased blood going to my brain.' A very smart guy called Jeremy

Jamieson deduced this. He's an eminent social psychologist from the University of Rochester in the United States and reframing how we see stress is his stock in trade – so much so that he has spent the better part of his career investigating the performance outcome of relabelling stressful situations.

An example: in one academic study those who were told to feel *positive* about feeling anxious increased their blood flow by an average of almost half a litre per minute. So what, you may think. So plenty. This basically means that retuning how you see a situation can result in more oxygen and energy running through your body. And that, in turn, will make you calmer and able to perform better, which is what the world's greatest athletes have known for a very long time.

FEAR AND THE GOLD-MEDAL-WINNING ATHLETE

Victoria Pendleton is not a fearful sort of person. She couldn't be. She is, after all, one of the most successful female British athletes of all time, with nine world titles and two gold medals to her name. She is regularly cited as one of the most talented professional cyclists of all time. She is, in that most hackneyed of phrases, a 'national treasure'; a woman who has devoted her life to her sport and, along the way, carried us along for the ride.

When she retired from the sport in 2012, the world thought that was it. She would, like so many athletes before her, find her way to the sports commentators' couch – an old, glorified animal put out to pasture. And besides ... wouldn't that be nice? No more merciless training. No more highly modified diets. No more press intrusion or performance anxiety before a big race? And sure, it would be – if you weren't Victoria Pendleton, because in 2015 she was ready for another challenge. She'd been retired for just shy of four years at that point and was approaching her thirty-fourth birthday. She'd dabbled in light entertainment (*Strictly Come Dancing*); done the commercial endorsements and endless adverts (Pantene, Hovis Bread, a range of bestselling Pendleton bicycles); and done her stint as a commentator. Then one morning, as she waited to board a flight to New Zealand, something she describes as 'the most outlandish and audacious proposal' arrived in her inbox. It was a challenge, set by an online bookmaker, for Pendleton to compete in the 2016 Foxhunter Chase at the Cheltenham Festival.

Cheltenham is a big deal – one of the grandest and most revered horse-racing courses in the world. The Foxhunter Chase, held on the last day of the festival, is a steeplechase race held over three miles and with twenty-two different jumps. It is as exciting to watch as it's formidable to take part in.

Victoria looked at the date. The race was in thirteen months' time. What's more, Pendleton had never ridden a horse in her life. Plus, there were other things to consider. The world of horse racing is a hard, often insular world. Newcomers are rarely welcome. She would be competing against some of the most seasoned jockeys in the country, on one of the most public stages. The risk of failure was great. The risk of a life-threatening injury even greater. It would require her to metaphorically saddle up and step into her discomfort zone.

She solicited the advice of those around her. 'Crazy' was what most people came back with. That or, 'It's a very dangerous game.' 'People of your age don't start riding,' one experienced rider told her, 'especially not race horses.' But then Pendleton had spent her career defying the odds. A slight, pretty young woman from Bedfordshire, an unremarkable backwater county sixty miles outside London, she was, she says, never taken as seriously as other athletes. She was 'not the right shape'. She lacked the bulky, weightlifter silhouette many believed was necessary to blast through such races as the keirin – an eight-lap sprint round the cycle track. She was too 'girly' others said. She liked clothes and make-up, and when she wasn't on the track she wore her hair long and blow dried. She was not, many believed, what a true, powerful athlete should look like. And yet . . .

So, one glacial British morning she set off to see the professionals, driving the short distance to a race track not far from where she lived. As she stood there in the fog, unable to see more than an arm's length in front of her, she heard them: half a dozen horses galloping down the track, the heavy beat of their hooves sending tremors through the ground. And then, finally they appeared, cutting through the gloaming like something from a Manet painting.

'It's an exhilarating noise to hear horses galloping towards you. It gets the heart racing and the adrenaline pumping. The hairs on the back of your neck stand on end,' she tells me. 'And I'm familiar with that feeling. I don't hate it. My experiences of being in that place make me comfortable with it. After all, you need that kind of stimulation in order to be your best physically and mentally.'

A few weeks later she signed on the dotted line.

Why would she do this? Why, after years of pushing herself deep into her discomfort zone, with competition after competition, would she choose to do it all over again – and this time in a sport she barely knew or understood? She did it because she knows how easy it can be to feel comfortable inside your dis-comfort zone. Victoria Pendleton has spent her life competing. She knows what it feels like to be consumed with nerves before a big race. She knows the rhythm of her own heartbeat. She knows that 'nerves' are all part of the success process.

'As a kid I found competitions overwhelming and unpleas-ant to be honest,' she tells me. 'Even now there are times in my career when the competition is almost traumatic, because I've wanted to succeed so desperately. But when it comes to competition you're always going to have those feelings. You need them. You *want* to have them. It's a natural instinct. Your body does it to look after you. You can't control them. They will always be there. You just need to better understand them and be familiar with them.'

In other words, you have to learn to get comfortable with the uncomfortable, otherwise you're on the path to 'discom-fort paralysis'. Part of that means reframing those feelings as advantageous rather than debilitating. 'I think you have to [reframe them] because if you are fearful and you give into it, then you're frozen most of the time. In sport the race will start at the time it's going to start and you just have to be on the start line. And those last few minutes before it happens . . . I am always slowing my heart rate down. My thoughts are run-ning wild and my heart feels like it's about to explode outside of my chest. I try to think: Keep calm. Experience it. Just kind of accept that you need it. You need that stimulation [to have] quick reaction speeds and good decision-making. So you need to be like: "C'mon. I'm ready." Rather than: "Oh God, I need the toilet. I'm panicking. My heart is going up my throat. I feel like I've got a thousand butterflies in my stomach and any minute now I might be sick." No, you need to recognise those feelings. You recognise them. You accept them. You rationalise that you need them.'

Pendleton, like most world-class athletes, has what I call 'discomfort recognition' down to a fine art. She reels off all the sensations most of us experience when we're in our discomfort zone as though she were giving me her name, age and date of birth. She can describe the way her skin tingles, how her heart races, the way the whole experience feels like a 'rush' that almost catches her out.

By understanding how her body reacts (and, of course, by repeated exposure to this feeling) she is never caught off guard. Because it's when we're caught out, when a great big adrenaline rush catches you like a surfer on a wave, that we freeze. That's the moment you are paralysed. That's the Daniel Day-Lewis moment. That's the 'discomfort paralysis' that stuffs it all up.

LEARNING TO LOVE DISCOMFORT

Remember those students who found themselves feeling challenged rather than terrified before taking their seats in the exam hall? That's the state you need to get to before your next big meeting/speech/whatever that you are dreading. Sports psychologists call it the 'challenge state' and it's exactly what Pendleton was talking about when she described her 'Let's do this' mindset before a race. But how do *you* get there?

Sports psychologists say you need three things to reach your 'challenge state'. One: the perceived notion that you are in control of the situation. Two: self-belief (no biggie then).

Three: your approach focus (in other words, do you aim to do your best or do you simply aim not to do your worst).

YOU'VE GOT TO THINK IT TO BE IT

Some people say you've got to see it to be it. I go one step further and say you've got to *think* it to be it. Great leaders and performers know this too, which is why they turn to visualisation to get them through their toughest challenges. They imagine what a successful outcome will look like before it's even happened. I call it montaging – kind of like playing a short film of your most amazing moments on a loop in your head. (Most of us have done this about someone we fancy at some point in our lives. You know, worked your way through all the best bits in your head, so that by the time you actually date them they're actually pretty dull.)

Let's say you're about to go for a job interview. Imagine what a successful job interview would look like. Maybe you'd walk in, smile, take the right seat, waltz through your CV and have quick-fire answers to even the gnarliest questions. When you go to leave, they'd look you in the eye, shake your hand and say: 'We'll be in touch', with all the sincerity of someone who is basically going to beg you to come and work for them by the end of the day.

Of course, most of us don't do this. But we do 'montage' – just in a completely different way. We 'negativise' everything. We envisage what said interview will look like, imagining only all the bad things that could happen. We visualise ourselves tripping up on entering the room. Taking the wrong seat.

Getting struck with 'discomfort paralysis' when asked tricky questions. Leaving the interview with little hope of a follow-up, because we have basically ballsed it up from the minute we walked in to the moment we left.

Montaging is a powerful thing, which is why catastrophising the outcome in our heads exacerbates our 'adrenaline reaction'. We think about all the mistakes we're about to make, which makes our hearts beat faster and our palms sweat more, which in turn leads us to panic more, which in turn leaves us frozen and basically screwed. Why? Because the part of your brain that is being used to project the (dismal) future outcome creates a stress response – a response that basically causes you to go into meltdown and, more crucially, means you can't engage in the moment.

But there is an answer – and it's way easier than you'd think. Simply imagine the outcome in a positive light and your body's reaction will change.

Take Wayne Rooney. Before every match the former England and Manchester United football captain used to ask the club's kit man what colours the team would be wearing the next day. Why? Because it helped him 'visualise'. Every extra detail that he could bring to his visualisation technique would impact his performance. 'I lie in bed the night before a game and imagine myself scoring goals and doing well,' he said during an interview. 'You're trying to put yourself in that moment and trying to prepare yourself . . . to have a memory before the game.' Rooney admitted he had done this his entire life – even as a small child. But what may have been instinctive to this young footballer is exactly what sports psychologists and coaches have been teaching their pupils for years.

Gold medal-winning heptathlete Jessica Ennis-Hill says she visualises her technique before a big tournament in the hope it will better affect her physical performance. Wimbledon champion Andy Murray has been known to go to an empty Centre Court and just sit there, imagining himself hitting balls over the net. One of Britain's all-time great rugby players, Jonny Wilkinson, goes one further and creates a multi-sensory mental image of his performance: 'You are creating the sights and sounds and smells, the atmosphere, the sensation and the nerves, right down to the early morning wake-up call and that feeling in your stomach. It helps your body to get used to performing under pressure.'

Vivid imagery not only prepares you, but can, studies show, affect your performance. I know, sounds like some weird voodoo magic, but simply imagining yourself succeeding in a situation can have a significant effect on the outcome. Of course, just imagining yourself acing an exam or carving a six-pack is not enough – you do need to put in the effort too. (That said, in a study by the Cleveland Clinic Foundation in Ohio, those who imagined themselves doing biceps curls five times a week for two weeks increased their strength by 13 per cent. Go figure.)

Envisioning yourself in a situation performing brilliantly can trigger neural firings in your muscles, creating a sort of mental blueprint from which your body can work to produce a better performance down the line.

So how can you do this? As you've seen from the examples we've gone through, the key is detail. Imagine you're a film director and your job is to create the most realistic mental montage of yourself as possible. How would you do that? How would you create so many layers that the image you have of yourself firing on all cylinders is so real, so nuanced, that by the time you came to actually perform you felt in complete control?

Set the scene

First start by visualising the scene. Most of us can do this. If it's a job interview, say, imagine what the office block looks like. Google maps mean most of us can now get scarily accurate images of pretty much any building we choose. What area is it in? What street is it on? Sounds borderline creepy but do street view. Take that little yellow Google person and virtually walk down the street. Take in the buildings around you, the scale of the street, the amount of traffic there. Sure, you could do an Andy Murray and hang around outside the building, but I'm not going to suggest that here, because loitering outside the building where you are potentially about to work is not a good look for anyone.

Keep adding detail as it comes to you. What are you wearing? What shoes do you have on? How do you have your hair that morning? All of this may not come to you straight away, so my advice is to start as early as possible, almost as soon as you have the interview pencilled into your diary. Then get imagining. You'll find it's actually a lot of fun.

Build the ambience

Next you need to create the sensory experiences around you. You can, of course, go into full-on method-acting mode. This would include creating actual smells and noises you may encounter on your way to said interview. But how you're going to create the idle banter of colleagues as you walk towards the interview room *and* the smell of someone's wilting vegetable lunch from the communal fridge is anyone's guess. No, you're going to have to dig deep into your imagination for this one. I always try to draw on past experiences. I try and imagine the colour of the office carpet (disclosure: it's almost always grey or hospital-coat blue). Then I try and build up the picture with the noises attached. If there's a water cooler (there is always a water cooler), imagine the gurgle it makes as the receptionist offers you a glass of water. And by the way, *always* accept the glass of water, even if you're not thirsty and are worried it will make you need the toilet. It takes your voice down by at least an octave. If you're struggling with this part, then try and aim for at least five associated sensory experiences. Any fewer and I tend to think you can't build up a realistic picture.

Get acting

This is the Jonny Wilkinson bit and some people find this easier to do than others. Sometimes just thinking about the event can trigger a nervous system response, so you may find your stomach doing backflips and your breathing becomes shallower as you imagine yourself sitting in front of your future boss being grilled like a Nando's chicken thigh. This is good – you can work with this.

Slow your breathing down. Count it out. Count slower and slower, making your breathing match the numbers. This should stop your heart beating like a jungle drum. It should also help your stomach relax. Hold on to this feeling, because every time you montage the scenario (and I'd suggest doing this at least three or four times before the big day, though you can do it as often as you like) try and recreate these feelings. It may sound like lunacy but remember, whether you like it or not, it is going to happen on the big day, so the best we can do is to prepare for it, so that when it does, you are quickly able to make the feeling subside rather than getting overwhelmed. You need to conserve all your energy for showboating just how exceptional you are, after all.

Write the script

For some people, writing this down helps. So go wild, write your own script. And I'm talking about old-school pen and paper by the way. Remember those? Studies show that the simple act of writing something down (not typing it on an iPhone or laptop) helps to lodge it in your memory. It's one of the reasons we tend to remember storylines and become more immersed in a book when we read it from a tangible paperback rather than an eReader. It also goes some way to explaining why book sales are increasing for the first time in years, while eReader sales are declining. It doesn't have to be *War and Peace* – you can break down your visualisation into chunks and just commit to paper the bits you think you'll struggle with on the day.

The one thing to remember when you are montaging is to be true to yourself. I know that sounds like some sort of half-baked Instagram quote, but I'm serious. There's no point in imagining yourself suddenly speaking with a deep voice if your own voice is higher pitched and soft. No point montaging yourself striding into a room with all the bombast of Don Draper if you're the quieter, more reserved sort. No point embellishing to the point of unrecognisability, because ultimately it will trip you up. No, make this montage true to who you are. Only then will you be able to inhabit it when the day comes.

What will montaging do for you? It's the surest way to guide you towards a 'challenge state' rather than one of 'discomfort paralysis' when things get tough. Remember how sports psychologists say you need three things in order to reach your challenge state: control, a positive approach focus and self-belief. Well, montaging can help you to achieve all three. Having a clear plan, one that you have rehearsed over and over again (even if only in your head), will automatically make you feel in control of the situation. Feeling in control of the situation and having a clear mental image of what a 'positive' outcome could look like will give you a positive approach focus.

As for the self-belief part . . . it's a nebulous old thing. The truth is, it's very hard to say to someone, 'You've got to have self-belief!', because, hell, wouldn't we all love to have it, and wouldn't it be lovely if there was a simple trick or tip that gave it to us. In my experience self-belief comes with practice: by practising the process and the outcome of whatever it is that you are terrified of, your self-belief will bubble to the surface.

As for Victoria Pendleton, when the day finally came – after months of practice, months of pressure from both the press and the horse-racing world, as well as months of near falls (and the occasional actual fall) – she was ready. She was ready to throw herself into her new discomfort zone. She blocked out the crowds, zoned out the fact it was a 450-kg beast beneath her and not a 7-kg bicycle and breathed. She listened to her body; she accepted that her quickening heartbeat was part of the process, not part of a problem. She leaned into it. She imagined crossing that finish line. She was comfortable with the sheer discomfort of it all. She was not only ready ... she was excited. And the result? She came fifth and described it as probably the greatest achievement of her life.

2

THE OBSTACLE ILLUSION

The danger of avoiding discomfort

I want to give you an idea of how much I used to like comfort. I was the classic middle child: quiet, deeply unremarkable, cushioned by all the failings and boundary-testing of my elder siblings before me, and spared the overindulgence bestowed upon my younger brother. As the third child of four I could slip under the radar. I was wrapped in a big comfy proverbial blanket and I didn't need to do very much to justify my existence.

A popular elder sister at school meant I was shielded from sharking bullies. A culture-nut older brother meant I was handed my taste in films, music and books as though a tray of sweets and told not to question them, just to swallow and accept that I would enjoy every one of them. Which I dutifully did. When my sister moved from Manchester down to London I followed, dog-like, five years later. I dressed the same way, spoke the same way, hung out with the same crowds, or should I say ... hung *around* the same crowds she hung out with. I basically spent the first eighteen years of my life being so comfortable, inhabiting a world so ready-made for me by everyone else that, as I slid out of my teens, I realised that not only did I have no idea of who I was, but I had no idea of who I *could* be. And so, on the eve of my twenty-first birthday, I did something radical. I moved to Paris.

The truth was I was sick of being somebody's 'little sister'. What had once been an easy and comfortable introduction into social situations was now an uncomfortable burden. It was charming to be introduced as someone's younger sibling when I was thirteen, fourteen, even sixteen. But at eighteen? I felt like a big infant, shielded by my elder sister's dazzling personality. People assumed we were the same. Even I assumed we were the same. Kind, older people would stop to talk to me at parties and realise pretty sharpish that I had very little to say other than to ape the opinions and affectations of my sister.

It dawned on me that I had to find out who I was. And that was scary. What if I didn't like who I was? What if my tastes were nothing like I had spent my life presuming they were? What if everything I had gone along with in my life was totally wrong for the 'real' me? The best and quickest way to answer these questions, I figured out, was to move to another city, with another language and where I knew *no one*. It was not that I was especially brave. It was that I was especially eager to find out in as short a time as possible who I might be. That, and the fact I had watched a lot of French films.

I remember stepping off the 9.07 a.m. Eurostar to Gard du Nord with a single black suitcase. I had little money, nowhere to stay and a job I had hooked up, teaching English in one of the toughest neighbourhoods in Paris. I pulled out the small plastic bag of francs that I had collected, tried – with the one line of French I had been practising for weeks on end to ask for a Metro ticket (it didn't work) – and then headed to my hostel deep in the centre of Paris. The hostel smelt of old cooking fat and the mellow fruitfulness of unwashed armpits. I was handed a key to my room in the way only the French can hand you a key (with a grunt and a finger that pointed in a vague direction towards the back of the building). I turned the key. The room was not the quaint, floral wallpapered garret of my imaginings but was a single box room painted a bright fleshy pink – kind of like a giant vulva – with a pair of bunk beds on which currently slept a person of unidentified sex/nationality.

I placed my bag on the bed, sat down and stared at the floor. I needed comfort. I went to find my packet of change to phone my mum and discovered it was gone. I didn't know how to make a reverse-charge phone call from France because I'd never had to do such a thing before. So I just sat there, my cheeks burning, holding back the overwhelming impulse to cry, because of course I couldn't do that with a complete stranger snoring above me. I had hit an obstacle. I had entered my discomfort zone without a roadmap to follow. And in that moment, I had two choices: stay in Paris and move forward *into* that obstacle. Or move around it, go back to England and seek the comfort of home.

I chose to stay. It wasn't an easy year, but it was a magical time of growth and challenge when I discovered things about myself. Turns out I could control a classroom of thirty rebellious teenagers (leadership skills emerge in the strangest places). I was way tougher than I had thought too. Alone, in a foreign country, with a terrifyingly small vocabulary, I learned the art of turning up alone to parties where I knew no one. (Grab a drink

THE OBSTACLE EVADER

This is a common reaction to an obstacle. In fact, I have used this technique many times throughout my own life. And I can tell you now: it's the one with the most disastrous outcome. Not immediately, but *ultimately*. Taking this approach to an obstacle is the one that will land you in the most trouble further down the line.

I'm going to give you an example of someone I know, whom I'm going to call Emily. At college Emily wanted to be a scriptwriter, and she got a pretty good headstart on a lot of us. Straight out of university, she landed a couple of internships working alongside some of the country's most well-known and respected writers. Sure, the pay was terrible and the hours crappy, but it was what she had always wanted to do. It was her grand passion! It was what she had dreamed about as a young girl writing plays for her troupe of Barbie dolls. It was what, in her heart, she felt she was 'destined' to be.

One day a full-time job came up on the writers' team she was assisting. It was between her and three other interns. She made her application in her own words 'shit hot'. And guess what? She didn't get it. What's more, her internship was up. She was going to have to go it alone. She spent a month calling round the few contacts she had made in the scriptwriting world. No one had any work. She had hit an obstacle. So what did she do? She cried. Then she got angry. She blamed the profession she had chosen for not spotting her talent and giving her the job. She then did the craziest thing of all: she decided she didn't want to be in scriptwriting anymore. It was 'too competitive' she said. And 'really badly paid'. And the people who worked in it 'not that smart anyway'. Far better to try her hand at journalism instead she decided.

So she started all over again. She got an internship and then, a few months later, landed a job as a junior writer on a nice little magazine. It wasn't better paid as it turned out, but she got to have her name in print every few months. And she got to interview smart, interesting men and women. But over time she got tired of the magazine. She wanted to write bigger features. She wanted to interview celebrities. Her boss told her she wasn't ready. So, guess what she did? She blamed the boss for not being 'encouraging' enough. And the job from 'holding' her back. Nine months into the job, she quit.

No matter, she told herself and everyone she knew: she was going to start a blog. If she was her own boss she could write whatever she wanted, when she wanted. And besides, she had heard bloggers were making good money for writing very little. But, like so many blogs, it didn't pay the bills. She blamed the timing: she had come to blogs too late in the day. It was a saturated market. No, the smart people were going to YouTube. So she set up a YouTube channel. But all that editing. All that filming. You know what's coming . . . she gave up.

The last time I saw her she was trying to set herself up as an 'influencer' with a beautifully curated Instagram account. She'd heard that brands were paying influencers thousands of pounds to endorse their products. I didn't break it to her that she would need at least a hundred thousand followers before she got the call from her 'favourite' protein brand. And by the time that happened, the world would probably have moved on to something else anyway.

Emily is what I call an Obstacle Evader. Instead of accepting the discomfort of the situation, she thought she'd outsmart it. She didn't have to deal with the rubbish pay of the scriptwriting business or the constant uncomfortable rejection because she left it altogether. And she didn't have to put up with her crabby, ambition-sapping boss at the magazine where she worked, because she could just go and be her own boss with her own blog. And video editing was so hard and laborious for so little reward ... far smarter to set up her 'brand' on Instagram where all you need is a flashy filter and a good phone camera.

She thought she had 'hacked' the system. Instead she had simply drifted further away from her goals and ambition. An obstacle is a deviation on your path to getting to where you want to get to. Obstacles may mean you change direction, but they shouldn't ever mean you change your entire path. What Emily did, time and time again, was completely change her course. By taking a new path (or, in her case, switching careers) it momentarily dodged the discomfort brought about by the obstacle in her path.

Great, you'd think. I don't have to deal with the associated anxiety and frustration the obstacle poses anymore. As if by magic I have made it disappear! But all you have done is created a much wider and more problematic obstacle. You have gone off on so many new horizontal paths, all leading you sideways rather than pushing you forward, that you have lost your way completely. If you leave it too long it can be difficult to ever find your way back, and it will take a lot more pain and anxiety and discomfort than the original obstacle you were running from in the first place.

THE OBSTACLE BLAMER

Another reason why human nature isn't too keen on obstacles: they teach us about ourselves – and not always nice things. They confront us with our limitations. Sometimes our weaknesses. Very often our failings. Now, if you're someone with supremely high self-esteem, that causes a problem. (We're not talking about healthy self-esteem here, by the way, but almost narcissistic levels. You and I both know these people.) Imagine it: your whole world view of yourself is brilliant. You have never even come close to failing. You coast through life. And then – hang on a minute. What is this? An obstacle? Something that means I'm going to struggle? Something that is going to make me feel deeply uncomfortable? To hell with this!

What often happens is that these people blame the *obstacle* for their lack of success. Far easier to do that than to look inward and accept failings or limitations on your part. In fact, some people will go one step further and put obstacles in front of the obstacle. (I know that's a pretty meta thing to get your head around.) Why? Well, because if you put a smaller obstacle in front of a bigger one then you never have to be confronted with true struggle. It's classic self-defeating behaviour. Maybe you've done it yourself on a smaller scale. I had an ex-colleague once who, whenever they were asked to take on a big project, would always hunt down a dozen little obstacles: they didn't have the right version of PowerPoint, they didn't have enough people to help them, there wasn't enough information to allow them to do the project properly ... so that they never had to face the real obstacle – completing the bigger project that had been asked of them. Look out for it; it's a common practice. And I'm not even sure those doing it understand what they're doing. All I can tell you is that ultimately it will trip them up.

What all obstacle blamers have in common is that they find fault with the obstacle rather than with themselves and their own limitations. And you know what? That's not a bad way to live. It means you spend your life thinking you're excellent and talented and a good person, mainly because you've never been tasked with challenging any of those self-imposed preconceptions. But here's where it stops being good: you never progress, and so you start to get angry. And frustrated. Because if you are all the things you think you are, then why are you standing still? Why are other people getting all these opportunities that you are not? Why are your friends getting promoted while you're still in the same crummy job? Why has no one spotted that you're a *smart, talented and highly employable person*?

The problem lies in those very words. You have never fully challenged yourself. Because if you had (and obstacles are life's way of giving you that opportunity), then you would probably have a more realistic view of what you're actually like. And that's crucial for moving forwards in the world. By the way, most people never get a true sense of their 'complete self' because they are too scared to see where their weaknesses are. These are the people who look back on their lives and tell themselves they didn't achieve what they could have because they were just 'unlucky'. Sure, that may make them sleep better in their coffins at the end of their days, but it also means they never took control of the direction of their own lives. You do not want to be this person.

Truly successful people explore their weaknesses just as much as their strengths (even more so in many cases). That's because, once they have a complete picture of who they are, they can make a life plan that will accommodate all of those attributes. (Or, as we'll see later in this book, work on their weakness so that they are prepared to tackle the life they really want.) So, how do you find out quickly what your weaknesses are? You guessed it: you need an obstacle. You need discomfort.

But that's not how the Obstacle Blamer sees it. Rather than accept any personal responsibility, what they do is fault the obstacle. Say there's a job you really *really* want. You get past the first interview, but then have to prepare a project for the next bit. The project is hard. You struggle. You stay awake at night wondering how you're going to do it. And that's a shock, because if you're as talented as you thought then you'd ace this surely? So, then you do one of two things:

1. You quit the next stage of the interview. The project was too demanding. It was unreasonable. They only set it so they could steal your brilliant ideas anyway. Who wants to be part of a company that operates like that? See: the obstacle's fault. *It* was too hard. *It* was unreasonable. *It* was not fair. All this, rather than thinking: 'This is hard, so I'm really going to stretch what I know now.' Or, 'It *is* a lot of work to ask for, but that will be a test of my dedication.' Or, 'Yes, they may steal my ideas, but far more likely they'll choose me for providing such great concepts. Even if I don't get this job, hopefully they'll remember me the next time around.' You get the idea.

of fear: there's the kind that can be utilised and galvanised into something positive and ultimately rewarding, and then there's fear that can crush you. The latter is the sort the Obstacle Magnifier gets caught up in. They become so frightened of what's in front of them that they not only abandon their path, but also let the obstacle colour everything they do thereafter.

I experienced this early on in my career. Back before I became a journalist I was a door-to-door saleswoman. The job was pitched to me as press and marketing assistant for a new drink's launch, but essentially it was selling a bunch of fermented Austrian cold drinks to department stores and bars. It was 2001, at which moment in time most people thought fermentation was something that happened when you left an egg sandwich in your school bag. (Ironically, fermented drinks are now the height of chic in hipster bars.) Still, I set out every morning with a box full of heavy glass bottles and a list of meetings I had set up with buyers across London. One day I turned up to a total of fifteen meetings, all scattered across town. Seven of those meetings never happened because the buyers weren't around. That, or they had forgotten or were 'too busy'. The final one made me wait for over an hour before I overheard them saying, 'can someone go and see that girl about those weird drinks'. In the end, the meeting lasted all of two minutes and it was with the Polish woman who worked the catering section and who, although lovely, understood about 17 per cent of what I was saying.

It was a pretty shitty experience for sure, but to my twenty-two-year-old self it was *everything*. I completely calamitised it, magnifying it to such a degree that I handed my notice in the very next week. It wasn't just that I told myself that I couldn't sell a bunch of fermented health drinks, I convinced myself that I couldn't sell – full stop. I magnified the day and my incapacity to sell anything to the degree that I vowed never, ever to work in sales in any capacity ever again. And I never did. Even up until recently, when any aspect of my job has come to close to selling I tended to avoid it. That one bad day clouded everything, for years. And I'm sure I missed out on some pretty epic opportunities because of that.

Whichever of these types you identify with – and chances are we all have a little of each of them – the bottom line is this: in order to grow, you have to get over the obstacle. There's a hard way to do that, which is to throw yourself straight into it, or there's another way. Interested? I thought so . . .

'Obstacles don't have to stop you. If you run into a wall, don't turn around and give up. Figure out how to climb it, go through it, or work around it.' That's basketball star Michael Jordan, one of the most successful athletes in American history, as well as sport's very own bard. (Seriously, put his name plus quote into Google and see the whole search engine light up with motivational sonnets.) Going through a wall or climbing over it is all well and good if you have the mental and physical constitution of an A-grade athlete. Grit and per-severance are hardwired into their DNA. But for the rest of us? We can take a *micro-deviation*.

THE MICRO-DEVIATION

So we've established what you don't do when you're confronted with an obstacle. You don't veer off your path. You don't give up your goal. You don't crumble under fear. Instead, you work your way around what is in front of you.

That's what Eric Underwood did. Eric, by the way, is one of the twenty-first century's greatest solo dancers, a man who has performed with everyone from the American Ballet Theatre in New York to the Royal Ballet in London, where, incidentally, he was the first black soloist. To look at him now, Eric Underwood is not a man who appears to have many obstacles in his path. He has had a long and bountiful career as one of the most successful dancers of his generation and, since leaving the Royal Ballet in 2017, has had an equally successful career as a fashion model, appearing on the front of Italian *Vogue* with Kate Moss, and is currently the global face of H&M. But ask him about obstacles and he'll tell you: obstacles have made him what he is today.

Eric's mother always knew her youngest son was destined for greatness. It wasn't that he showed any particular flair for acting, or even any great aptitude for dance (although, when Saturday night rolled around and she broke out the Al Green and Marvin Gaye LPs, that kid could *move*). No, she knew her son Eric was going places because she was going to teach him something that he would use for the rest of his life. She was going to show him that in order to get along in life you just had to understand one thing: that when you came up against an obstacle, there was *always* a way around it.

This was important, because the Underwoods encountered obstacles around them day in day out. Eric grew up in a tough neighbourhood on the outskirts of Washington D.C. – a place where gangs were rife and the sounds of gun shots and police sirens pierced the evening air.

One night a young police officer came to the Underwoods' door. A man had been murdered outside the apartment block where they lived. Had they seen anything? Eric's mother shook her head. She had done and *would* do everything in her power to make sure her family were not affected by the chaos outside her door. At weekends the old Soul records she would play when she pushed back the furniture to make a dance floor for the kids drowned out the sirens. And when the sound of guns being fired outside got too bad she would bring the children into her room at the back of the apartment and make them lie very low and still on the floor. The crime-ridden suburb into which Eric had been born was its own giant obstacle, but Mrs Underwood wasn't going to let that stop her children going places.

A performing arts school not far from where they lived was a ticket out for young Eric. He was an animated child with a vivid imagination. At home he was forever putting on fashion shows or amateur plays he had written. So his mother had an idea: she would make sure Eric got into this school, rather than the tougher public school down the road. She marched him to the local library, found a monologue in a book about a young boy in a wheelchair and made Eric learn every line off by heart. When the school's acting auditions came round she sent fourteen-year-old Eric off with a kiss, a smile and a prayer.

But when he got to the audition something terrible happened. He got 'discomfort paralysis' and blanked halfway through the audition. The teachers waited. And waited. Time seemed to stand still. And then he heard it, delivered with all the compassion of a reality star judge. 'I'm sorry Eric . . . this just isn't for you.' This is the point where most of us would grab our bags, hold back the tears, blame ourselves (or the teachers, let's be honest, for failing to grasp our potential) and rethink our entire performing arts career. But that's not what Eric Underwood did.

'I remember as soon as they said, "This isn't for you", I walked out thinking – "Okay, it's not for me, so onto the next thing." And then, before I could even get that thought out of my head I saw a couple of girls doing splits getting ready for a dance audition that was about to happen. I had on jean shorts and so I hiked them up and joined in. I thought, "Well, I'll give it a go and see what happens. And if this doesn't work out then I'm going to try and become a painter. I'm going to be here all day auditioning if that's what it takes."'

What Eric demonstrated that day – and what he went on to demonstrate throughout his entire dance career – was an unusual but highly effective response to obstacles. I call this Obstacle Blindness: he didn't see them. He saw only paths through them or round them. And so, when he saw the line of young girls limbering up for a dance audition, he saw his path through. Remember, Eric's obstacle was not getting into the acting class his mom had hoped he would. But the end goal was not to get into *acting* class; it was to get into the performing arts school. So he looked around (in his case it took minutes, for most of us it'll take a little longer) and thought about how he could come at the obstacle from a different angle. That different angle was gaining entrance to the school via another avenue: dance.

There is fourteen-year-old Eric in his jeans rolled high

up to his thighs, surrounded by young ballerinas who have been stretching and pirouetting since they were three years old. The teacher turns to this scrawny kid who is standing in the doorway asking to audition and she says: 'I'm sorry, it's for trained dancers only.' Another obstacle thrown his way almost immediately. 'So I turned to her and I said, "If you show me I can do it." So she put me on the floor and she checked that I could do a split and I guess because I was the only guy they were intrigued. Then she said: "Okay, try it out. You're far behind but we'll try it." And to me that was *it*.'

But *it* wasn't easy. To say Eric was 'far behind' was an understatement. He was fourteen years old. He had never had a formal dancing lesson in his life. He knew he could move, but that was it. One day, three weeks into his time there, one young girl turned to him and said: 'Eric, why can't you just *dance*?'

'I was really frustrated with myself because I was thinking the exact same thing,' he tells me. 'The teacher would say to me: "You have the flexibility. You have the ability to jump. You have the balance." But I didn't have the coordination. I knew street dance. I could move, but I didn't have posture and I didn't know how to hold myself.' Obstacle number three: how do you make up eleven years of technique in a matter of months? Not only this: how do you come to terms with this huge, seemingly insurmountable obstacle without crumbling?

I asked Eric. 'Well the difference when you're fourteen and someone says "This is right, this is wrong" is it's really easy to achieve, right, because you become obsessed and it's really clear. When you're three years old you're just mimicking what someone's doing, but without a clue as to why you're doing it. So, at fourteen I felt I had an advantage in the sense that I understood what I was trying to achieve.'

We have already established that obstacles are hard – that's the point. They are a test to see what you're made of. I always think most people are much stronger and more capable than they ever thought possible. The issue is, most people never get to see that because they are not prepared to take the difficult, obstacle-strewn journey to find this out about themselves.

Even taking a micro-deviation is not easy. It will be easier than blasting through the obstacle, but it will test you. What you have to do is give it positive meaning. In Eric's case, the micro-deviation was getting into the dance class as a means to getting into the school. Once he had done that, however, he was still faced with an obstacle. Now this was a far less overwhelming obstacle than failing to get into the acting class, but it was an obstacle all the same. For, while Eric was good enough to be there, he had almost a decade *less* of a dance education than everyone else in that class. At this point, he could have become one of the three types we have already outlined. He could have deemed the new obstacle too big, blamed it and walked out (the Obstacle Blamer). He could just as easily have adopted the Obstacle Evader mindset and decided midway that he no longer wanted to be a dancer or, indeed, to be at that school. Or he could have become so consumed with fear, like the Obstacle Magnifier, that he would have been unable to continue with the course. All three of those mindsets would have resulted in the same thing: Eric quitting the class.

Instead, he did something miraculous. He took control of the obstacle by giving it *positive* meaning. He realised that coming to a discipline as difficult as dance so late in the day could be deemed beneficial. After all, infants who are forced into ballet classes aged three by their parents seldom have the same desire for learning. Being older meant he could learn quicker and be more engaged. By arming himself with this knowledge he was able to not only provide comfort for himself while tackling this obstacle, but he was also able to give himself a very clear template of how to manoeuvre around it. Had he not done this he would have felt lost and out of control. And it's when we feel like this that we adopt one of the aforementioned mindsets.

Eric was able to throw himself into his training in a way other classmates could not. He felt he was at the perfect point in his life to absorb new information and learn how to dance technically. He worked. He worked day and night. As soon as he had done his homework he would disappear to his bedroom with his friend Marcia, throw his legs up against his bunk bed and get her to push down until he was in a full stretch. He would dance from the moment he got in until the moment he went to bed. And he was able to do this because he believed he was at the right point in his life to do it. Had he not told himself this, it's doubtful he would have pushed himself in quite the same way: 'I'd go to bed either stretching or thinking about dance and then I'd wake up excited to have another day where I got the opportunity to get better at this one step that I couldn't quite master.'

Dance, by its very nature, is an obstacle-laden pursuit. Dancers are set difficult, almost seemingly unattainable challenges very early on in their careers – multiple pirouettes, say, or grand jetés. These are movements the body is not naturally designed for, and in order to achieve them dancers must be fearless in their approach. So how did Eric do that? Well, again, he imbued each move he was tasked to perform with positive meaning. In Eric's case, he relished every unsuccessful jump and micro-failure on the dance floor, because it allowed him to see where he went wrong. He saw it not as failure but as opportunity. (Interestingly, he told me that he would write down every move he failed at, in order to better process why it had occurred.)

'You have to push yourself very hard in dance', says Eric. 'One day I'd go in and do a pirouette and fall over, and then maybe six months later I could do sort of one and half, and then maybe two years later I could do four. You have to accept that it's never going to be right. It's consistent failure. And the one day you get it right, it stops being exciting.'

One thing we'll come to see over the course of this book is that brilliant people do not see obstacles as painful upheaval. They see obstacles as invigorating challenge. When I asked everyone in this book what their greatest 'problems' were on the way to their success, they all struggled to give me an answer. Why? Surely it wasn't that their lives had been without problems and stress? No, it was that they never chose to see anything as a problem or an obstacle. They implicitly understood that discomfort was part of the process towards greatness.

THE OBSTACLE ILLUSION IN PRACTICE

Know what is on the other side

All this practice is rendered useless if you don't have one thing very clear in your mind before you set out on your obstacle-strewn course: your goal. What is it that lies on the other side of the obstacle/obstacles you are going to face? Because you need to be very clear about that. And you need to be very specific. Saying: 'I want to be successful' is too vague. You're not going to be able to come up with a plan or micro-deviation to get to where you want to go. Unless you know exactly where you want to be, your journey will be a lot harder.

Where do you want to be ...
in a month, in a year, in three years?

Sometimes it's too hard to know where you want to be in twenty years' time. Some people are lucky: they know exactly what they want to be and never deviate from that path. For most of us, though, life is a constant exploration of where we want to end up. And it changes all the time.

Break it down and ask yourself where you want to be in a specific time frame. Start by thinking about your immediate goals. For example: you want to be able to leave work earlier every night by the end of next month. Great, so what is the obstacle that is currently stopping you from doing that? Maybe it's that you spend the first hour of the day chatting with your colleague instead of putting your head down. Switch it around. Talk to her on the way out or the way home instead. Maybe you leave the hardest bit of work until the end of the day, so when you get to that it takes you twice as long as you thought. Okay, so move it to the front of your to-do list. Maybe you promise yourself you can't go home until you've finished your to-do list. If that never happens, then the obstacle may be that your to-do list is too long. Think about cutting it by a third and then see if you can finish it. These are all micro-deviations, but we can only think of them if we can identify where we want to be. By knowing that, we will quickly see the obstacles in our way. (And remember, obstacles are not always obvious.)

Do this again but use a different time frame next – six months or a year. Where do you want to see yourself? Got the answer? What is the main thing stopping you from getting there? Examine it in the same way we did above. You'll be amazed how quickly you will come up with answers. The human spirit and mind finds it much easier to come up with small, manageable solutions than grand ones.

Once you've done this, move the time frame again. Keep doing this until you feel like you have a plan of where you're going in the next three years. If you think you can imagine even further into your life then great, but three years tends to be a realistic time frame. I, for example, couldn't imagine what I'll be doing in ten years' time, but three years seems just close enough to vividly imagine the life I might have.

A word of caution here: try and think about what the *main* obstacle is when you're doing this exercise. If you come up with a long list you're never going to feel ready to tackle it. It will feel too overwhelming – like an attack by a small army rather than one giant foe. And besides, most of those smaller obstacles will be masking one major one. Let's say your ambition in three years' time is to own your own home. The obstacles you come up with are: 'I don't earn enough money.' Or, 'My rent is so high, I can't save.' Or, 'I've got too many other financial commitments at the minute.' These are all the same obstacle: 'You need to take control of your money.' Recognise that many small obstacles are often a shield for a major one you've been avoiding for a while.

GIVE DISCOMFORT MEANING

Remember how Eric reinterpreted his struggle in the beginning? How he told himself that he had an advantage over his fellow dancers, despite the fact they had been training for many more years? How he believed starting from scratch later in life was actually beneficial, because your body and mind were ready to learn? Well, that's what you're going to do from now on.

Once you've identified where you want to be and the obstacle you have to overcome in order to get there, you need to get through the hard yards you're going to face. Even the best book in the world can't tell you how to make an uncomfortable situation comfortable. But what I can tell you is that you can build a mindset that means you are better equipped to deal with that discomfort. One of those ways is to endow the experience with positive meaning. 'How do you do that?' I hear you ask. Easy, you need to ask yourself one question: Why am I the best person to be going through this now?

This forces you to look at all the positives you possess in order to fight the discomfort you're about to go through. If we use the example of saving for a house deposit for example, usually we would look at ourselves and think of all the reasons why it's the worst point in our life to take on this obstacle: you're not earning enough, you're dating so need money to go out, the housing market is crazy, yada yada.

But now think about why it could actually be the best time. Maybe you don't have the responsibility of children yet. Maybe you're single, so you don't have to take another person's choice about houses into consideration. Maybe, because you're younger, you can work longer hours or take on a second job as you're in the best health of your life. The list could go on and on. What is essential is that you see meaning in your struggle. This way you can go into an unknowable situation feeling empowered rather than frightened.

3

FROM TRAUMA TO TRIUMPH

The transformative power of major discomfort

At some point in your life things will fall apart. Quite without knowing why, your life will feel as though it has been ripped open at the seams and that there is no possible way of sewing it back together. It will be a situation that goes beyond simple discomfort. It is called major discomfort and it is a son of a real bitch. But, if you harness it in the right way it can also be one of the greatest opportunities you will ever be given.

In this chapter we will meet people who have experienced major discomfort, often more than once in their lifetime. Things have happened to them that most of us could never even contemplate and yet it is the very thing that has allowed them not only to grow as people, but also to transform the world around them. These are people who have waded into major discomfort like a fishing boat sailing into the eye of a storm. And in doing so they have emerged not as victims, not even as survivors, but as heroes, heroes who understand the power of huge, disruptive discomfort to make truly dramatic change.

What do I mean by 'major discomfort'? It's different for everyone. It could be the loss of a loved one; it could be a break-up; it could be a monumental mess-up at work; or even something as seemingly insignificant (to the rest of the world at least) as a mini public failure – a speech that goes wrong or a joke that falls flat in front of a crowd of people you admire. The point is that it leaves you traumatised.

Traumatising discomfort is the sort of discomfort that you can't prepare for. It's the sort that charges at you out of nowhere. When it hits you feel out of control. This isn't about stepping into your discomfort zone as much as it is your discomfort zone trampling all over you. You don't have time for a plan. And you don't have a chance to think things through. This is one of those times in your life when you get thrown a punch, and how you deal with it determines whether you transform or you crumble.

Trauma does not go away unless you transform it into something else. Trauma left to its own devices lingers, sending out tiny ripples that swell with time after the moment of impact. It does not go away by trying to forget about it. In fact, it only gets worse.

Of course, when something rocks us, the last thing we want to do is revisit it. Who wants to go over a traumatic experience? That's concentrated discomfort. But sometimes it's the only thing that works.

Let me give you an example from early on in my career. Granted, it was not a break-up or losing a loved one that left me devastated, but, as a naïve twenty-four-year-old, it was traumatic to me. I had landed my first job on a women's magazine. It had taken me years to get to that place – months and months of unpaid work experience, weeks of further unpaid writing gigs (journalism is nothing if not a financial succubus) and literally years of pestering anyone on a magazine masthead to give me a job. Finally, I had my 'in'. It was on an older women's magazine, the sort of thing my mother's friends would read. But it was vaguely glossy and the stories were interesting and meaty. There were beauty pages on how to tame crow's feet and fashion shoots with lots of voluminous clothing and sensible footwear. There were features on things like the perimenopause (honest to God, I thought this was a type of houseplant when I was first asked to research it) and empty-nesters piecing their lives back together after their children had flown. (Not knowing, of course, that they'd all be back by 2018.)

My job was mainly to interview women for a section of the magazine called 'Living the Dream'. The idea was that these women had all faced some sort of major discomfort that had affected them so deeply they had felt compelled to change the way they lived their lives. The stimulus was usually a swivel-eyed husband of thirty years who had spent the last decade of their marriage getting horizontal with his PA. But no matter what the catalyst, the upshot was always the same: they found renewed meaning in their lives after it happened, usually by starting a business and making shedloads of money.

My job was to interview them. And boy did I love it. I basically spent the first six months of my journalistic career asking the world's nosiest questions ('How much did you make in your first year?', 'How do you think your husband feels now?', 'Can you remember how you found out about your husband and the PA?') and getting paid to write about it. The problem was, it was only one half of my job. The other bit of it was being the administrative assistant for my entire department. There were invoices to process, trains to book, meetings to pop in diaries and newspapers to file. Except I didn't give too much thought to this part of my job, which is where the problems started.

I think it was the first day back after a holiday when I was summoned to my editor's office. Stupid me thought I was about to get a promotion (self-delusion can be a wonderful thing), that is, until I saw she was leading me into a small side office that was rarely used. She sat me down and basically told me this: I was not up to scratch. There were missing invoices, train tickets not booked and angry writers moaning about not being able to pay their mortgages because of the idiot girl whose job it was to process it all. It was simple, she said through a thin smile. 'You've got three weeks to improve and then . . . ' It was left hanging in the air like a bird of prey.

I was floored. I walked back to my seat in a daze. The whole office seemed to freeze in time. It felt like I was snorkelling through treacle. My breath caught, my cheeks burned and I had to clench my teeth to stop myself from crying in front of the entire room. I had just had my twenty-fourth birthday. With the salary from this job I had finally been able to move out of my sister's box room. I could at long last afford a supermarket shop. The cashpoint no longer flashed up *insufficient funds* every time I tried to use it. I was a journalist. I was going somewhere. But in that moment, it felt as though it was all about to be taken away. This was my major moment of discomfort.

Melodramatic? Sure. But I was a kid, alone in a city with few friends and no one I could really confide in. I was too ashamed to tell my parents. And God forbid I shared my load with anyone at work. To me, at that moment in my life, it was traumatic. And I had three options. A: Give in, shut myself away and accept that maybe I just wasn't cut out to be a journalist after all. B: Leave, but tell myself that this was their issue not mine. C: Wade back into the discomfort – understand why it had happened and how I could not only move on with it, but move *forward* with it.

I've always been a big diary writer. Ever since my mum bought me a pale-blue Winnie-the-Pooh journal I've turned to paper and pen to help make sense of a lot of my life: puberty, boys, friendships, men, career. For me diarising is a process rather than an art form. It's a place where I can organise my thoughts. That's what I did then, and what I still do today.

I still have the diary. It's funny to read it back now. On the day it happened you can literally feel the vitriol exuding from the page: 'I *hate* this place! Cannot believe I could lose my job because of this!' The next day's entry is sadder, more measured, but also full of gloom: 'I don't think they've ever got me at that place. I'm just too different. Maybe I'm too different to even be a journalist.' But as the diary extracts go on, what I notice is this: the language becomes less inflammatory, with fewer dramatic statements and more considered thoughts. It's also more organised. Whereas the first few entries are a jumble of highly emotional thoughts with no structure or timeline, they gradually settle into a more coherent, structured format. The very best bit is this: it becomes less about the problem with other people ('*She* doesn't understand me. *She's* too harsh') and more introspective ('I think I might be too disorganised; I feel a bit out of my depth some of the time').

Bit by bit, through writing the diary, I started to pick apart where I had gone wrong. And the more I analysed it, the more I understood the true nature of what had actually caused this period of major discomfort: sure, I was creative, but when I looked back over all the things I had been doing – sitting on invoices, putting organisational duties like booking train tickets to the back of my to-do list – I realised I was also woefully disorganised, something I had never realised about myself before. If you'd have asked me if I was a disorganised person I would have said no. My life wasn't particularly chaotic. I was punctual, my bedroom was immaculate, there were enough outward signs in my life to convince myself that I was a relatively 'together' person. Until disaster struck. Diarising in this way not only helped me make sense of the major discomfort that I was going through, but made me grow as a person by delving into aspects of my life that ordinarily I would never have questioned.

While I didn't realise it at the time, I was practising what scientists now believe is one of the most effective ways to deal with periods of major trauma and discomfort.

James Pennebaker is an academic from the University of Texas and has been fascinated by how people deal with traumatic fallout for most of his entire life. This is why he created a landmark study looking at how those who had suffered trauma in childhood, and had kept it a secret, fared later in life. The results were intriguing. In brief: those who had not spoken about the incidents that affected them as a child reported significantly greater health problems as adults.

Pennebaker was so amazed by this that he took the experiment one step further and, over a thirty-year period, asked people to come to his lab for fifteen minutes every day for three to four days and write about 'the most upsetting experience' of their lives. The experiences of those who took part varied greatly, from those who had been mugged or beaten up to those who had been raped or had attempted suicide. What constitutes a 'major discomfort' varies from person to person, but the effects of speaking about those traumas did not. Pennebaker found that those who had written down how they felt reported fewer visits to the doctors, reduced anxiety and depression, better grades and a better-functioning immune system.

Magic? Well, kind of. It turns out that writing (or even talking) about difficult experiences offers its own sort of voodoo powers. Here's how it works: by exploring what had happened to them the subject was able to grow wiser about the trauma through a number of unconscious steps. Firstly, Pennebaker found that, as the experiment went on, participants started to use words like 'I realise' or 'I understand', thereby showing greater insight into what happened to them. Next, they started to shift their perspective by moving from using the pronoun 'I' to 'he' or 'she', as in 'he attacked me' or 'she shouted at me'. What this showed was a greater distance being created between the individual and the trauma. Finally, Pennebaker found that those who were the most expressive with their writing – the ones who really let go, were the ones who came away acknowledging that the trauma had allowed them to find positive meaning in their lives.

While you can in no way compare my near-sacking to the

mammoth trauma these people faced, what I can say is this: expressing how I felt about it did give me my own sort of positive meaning. Exploring what *exactly* went wrong helped me understand office dynamics. Now, as an editor of a magazine, a red flag I always watch for is when a junior colleague goes quiet on a project. It's an instinct only I am sensitive to, and that is because I lived through it. (And nine times out of ten, silence usually indicates a problem someone is not coping with.)

You see major discomfort, if treated correctly, can be incredibly useful. Working through why something went wrong is painful, sure, but it's also an opportunity to process what went wrong. Often, when we go through a tough experience, we like to pop it in a box, shove it in a mental corner and move on quickly. But the problem with that is that the box always exists. What's more, there's just a jumbled mix of traumatic emotions in there, which you have never pieced together into a coherent story. The mind likes coherence. It likes to make sense of things, so that if something like it ever happens again, you're prepared. The exploration of major discomfort, therefore, particularly through writing, is an opportunity for us to become stronger in the face of further discomfort should it ever be repeated.

In the mid-nineties, two American scientists from the University of North Carolina, Richard Tedeschi and Lawrence Calhoun, discovered this for themselves. After studying a large group of bereaved parents for over a decade (as well as many other survivors of intense trauma) they found that major discomfort did not always affect them in the way they had been led to believe. In fact, rather than each one of them being only negatively affected by their experiences, all of them had also been affected in profoundly positive ways as well. They reported having better relationships as a consequence, discovering for the first time in their lives a sense of purpose and, perhaps most crucially of all, admitting to having developed a very resilient inner strength. Tedeschi and Calhoun were so amazed that people did not, in fact, crumble in the face of traumatic major discomfort, and instead thrived, that they gave it a name: post-traumatic growth (PTG).

Now, I know what you're thinking. This is crazy. If this happened, then why have so few people heard of it. Why, then, are we all so familiar with the term post-traumatic stress disorder (PTSD), an anxiety disorder caused by traumatic experience, which can manifest itself in myriad ways, from flashbacks to incapacitating depression.

That's because modern psychology has taught us that most people are *negatively* affected by major moments of discomfort. Think about it: have you ever heard anyone who was attacked or imprisoned come out and declare: 'Wow, that was the best thing that ever happened to me! I feel a stronger, more insightful person for having gone through that.' No, you do not. (And that's kind of a good thing when you think about it. After all, if we were to promote the psychological benefits of putting yourself through a whole heap of pain, God knows where we'd be.) What's more, we are bombarded by news stories supporting this train of thought: poor young soldiers now living on the streets because the stress of war has debilitated them to the point of no longer being able to interact with society. Emotionally devastated victims of sexual abuse who struggle to form long-term relationships. Angry young men and women incarcerated in children's homes because of domestic abuse who live for ever on the margins of society.

And yet, while these stories are indeed devastating, and the consequences for some sadly life-threatening, this is not the whole story for everyone. Researchers have discovered that, contrary to popular belief, almost two thirds of those affected by trauma experience growth, not stress, as a by-product. (The two are not mutually exclusive, however. You could experience PTSD *and* PTG.)

How, then, do you make sure you experience PTG after a period of major discomfort? To understand that I want you to meet someone.

Sajda Mughal was the sort of woman who had everything in order: a boyfriend on the brink of qualifying as 'husband material', a promising career as a recruitment consultant in a top investment bank, and a wardrobe filled with the sort of flashy bags and expensive shoes a teenage Sajda could have only dreamed about. But one hazy day in July 2005 she wasn't feeling so together.

It was a Thursday and she'd woken up late. She threw on her black work suit, grabbed her bag and raced to the nearest tube station, Wood Green, in North London. It was shut. Panicking, she made the ten-minute walk to the next-closest station, Turnpike Lane. That morning there were severe delays on the Piccadilly line, one of London's most congested tube tributaries taking commuters right into the heart of the capital. The platform heaved with men and women sweltering in the morning heat that was already making the underground feel like a mini furnace.

Sajda looked around. For the last couple of years, no matter what, she had always sat in the first carriage of every train she took. She put it down to the mild OCD that had been gathering pace over the last few years. But that day, for reasons she did not quite understand, she decided against it. Instead, when the doors opened and the crowds piled into the 8.48 am train from Cockfosters, she allowed herself to be swept into the middle carriage.

For the next ten minutes, as the train made its way into central London, newspapers rustled on commuters' laps, overexcited foreign students peered over maps of London, and a pregnant woman opposite Sajda shuffled in her seat to try and get comfortable. All Sajda Mughal could think was: 'I'm late. *Again.*' The train pulled out of King's Cross station and rushed into the darkness of the underground tunnel and then . . . BANG. A noise and a rush so forceful that the whole train shook like a dice. Those that were standing fell to the ground, or on top of those who were seated. The lights went out. The entire carriage fell silent.

Over the next few minutes several things happened. First the emergency lights flickered into action, casting a dim light over the train. Then slowly, almost imperceptibly at first, a thick black smoke started to creep under the carriage doors causing the entire train to heat up to over forty degrees within seconds. No one knew what had happened exactly, except that it was clearly something terrible. And it was then, in that moment, as Sajda took off her jacket and held it to her face to protect it from the thickening smoke, that she decided: today is the day I'm going to die.

'In my head we had derailed,' she tells me in her soft North

London accent. 'I thought, Oh my gosh, we have just left King's Cross at rush hour and in another minute a train is going to come our way and hit us. There's going to be a massive fireball and we are all going to be burnt to death.'

I asked her if she could remember her moment of major discomfort, when she believed her time was up. 'First of all, my heart felt like it had a rope around it that had been pulled so tight I could hardly breathe. Next, I started to have this trail of thoughts of everything I hadn't done with my life. I hadn't said bye to my mum or my siblings. I hadn't said bye to my boyfriend. I hadn't got married or had children or travelled the world. And then something weird happened, which I get emotional even thinking about now. I started to get all these old, happy memories flooding back: me at school, me playing with my father when he was still alive and when I was just a little girl.' There is a silence. 'And then I remember focusing on the date and thinking: So this is it then: "July 7th 2005. This is the day I will die."'

We now all know this day as 7/7 – a day of major trauma, not only for the hundreds of men and women who were caught up in the multiple terrorist attacks on that day, but for the entire city of London. Fifty-six lives were lost that day at the hands of four young terrorists who had travelled down from various corners of the UK with one thing in mind: to serve London its own kind of 9/11. Sajda Mughal, however, didn't find out until much later that day what exactly had happened. It was only that evening, as she sat in the semi-darkness of her mother's front room with the curtains drawn around her, that she heard the word 'bomb' followed by 'Islamic terrorists'.

Days later, as she pieced everything together, she would discover that a nineteen-year-old man named Germaine Lindsay had walked onto the first carriage of the train in which she was travelling that day at King's Cross. He had waited just a few seconds, until the train pulled out of the station and into the tunnel that linked it to nearby Russell Square, and then he had detonated the several pounds of explosives he had strapped to the inside of his rucksack. Twenty-six people died on Sajda's train. Most of them had been sitting in the front carriage, the exact place where Sajda had sat every single morning for the previous two years.

It's been over a decade since 7/7 and yet Sajda is still affected. She still remembers with absolute clarity the blood from the bodies on the platform as she was pulled up to safety from the rail tracks that day. She can still taste the smoke from the carriage. She can still recall the loud, shrill screams of those on the train, as well as the duller, softer moans of young men and women whispering: 'I don't want to die. I don't want to die.' She can still see the pregnant woman sat opposite, eyes closed, slumped peacefully in her seat. She tells me that, as the anniversary approaches each year, she talks in her sleep. Her husband hears her. She relives the moment she thought she was going to die, he tells her, repeating the names of all those she had not said goodbye to and all the things she had not yet done with her life.

And yet, ironically, the effects of 7/7 have also had an extraordinary effect on her life. That's because Sajda now runs one of the most important NGOs in the country: The JAN Trust. It's a charity dedicated to fighting and preventing extremism in the UK and its work has been so instrumental that in 2014 Sajda Mughal became Sajda Mughal OBE. Her days are now spent crossing the country to reach parents, siblings and even friends who suspect that those close to them are at risk of being recruited into extremist terrorist groups. She talks to young men and women, some as young as fourteen and fifteen, who are on the precipice of running to Syria to join ISIS as child fighters or ISIS brides. It is not easy. Every day she must step into her discomfort zone. She has had violent threats made against her for the work she does, both from those she is trying to protect and far-right extremists. Her office has been vandalised, hate mail posted through her door and her life has been threatened time and time again. And yet, when you ask her why she does it, her answer is, why wouldn't she?

That is because she is one of those who found strength from what happened on 7 July 2005. She knows others who were on the train that day whose lives have splintered in very different directions. Many are on antidepressants, she tells me. Probably for the rest of their lives. Others are too scared to step outside their homes. And then there are those who, to this day, find it almost impossible to talk about what happened.

'If 7/7 had not happened I would have had a very different life. I would have married later. Had kids later. My life before 7/7 was preoccupied with making money and having a good life. I wanted to buy shoes and handbags. It was a very self-orientated way of living. What happened on 7/7 changed everything.'

Her life has certainly been enriched since 7/7. Her relationships are stronger, she tells me – she married her husband two years after the bombing and had two children before she was thirty. She is stronger as a person and, she says, finds greater meaning in her life.

'Before 7/7 I was very stuck in my thoughts. But what happened to me that day gave my life a new sort of meaning. I can honestly say that without 7/7 having happened to me I don't feel I would be making the difference I am today.'

What made Sajda grow from her major discomfort where others diminished? She waded into it. Though she didn't write anything down, from day one Sajda has, she tells me, been very vocal about what happened: to friends, family and even strangers who had wanted to know more. The first question she says she asked herself when she discovered what had taken place on the morning of 7/7 was not, 'Why did this happen to me?' but 'Why did these young men do this?' (Sajda is herself from a devout Islamic background). Her work, of course, has allowed her to answer this question, but it has also allowed her to ruminate on what happened to her. It's no coincidence that Sajda's job running the JAN Trust means she must speak about 7/7 almost every single day. The interviews she has given to newspapers and books like this one means she also reads back her words time and time again. And while that doesn't lessen the pain of what happened that day, it has helped to transform her into a braver, stronger woman.

'I often question why I didn't get on that first carriage that day. I often question why I survived when others didn't. And I rationalised that I was given a sort of second chance. The whole 7/7 experience has been a journey, but I've also put myself on a journey – questioning everything that has happened. And I think because of that I am a stronger person. I would never have been able to public speak had this event not happened to me. I would never have been able to continue with the work I do, in the face of constant abuse and threats, if this hadn't happened to me.'

There are many others like Sajda who, although left devastated by their moments of trauma, have gone on to change the world as a consequence. I give you Baroness Doreen Lawrence, one of the foremost leaders and thinkers on race reformations in the UK. In March 1993 Doreen was a churchgoing mother to three children. She was remarkable only in her intense ambition for her two sons and daughter, that she made mealtimes with the family a priority and that she rationed the household television time. But on 22 April 1993 everything changed. Her eldest son, Stephen, was murdered by five white youths as he waited at a bus stop in South-East London. To lose a child is one thing, but the murder of Stephen Lawrence was exacerbated by bungled evidence, police errors and institutional racism.

The case became famous not only for the horrific nature of the crime, but also for the horrific treatment of British black men and women that it consequently unearthed. And yet . . . while she mourned for the loss of her eldest son, Doreen Lawrence somehow also found the strength to fight. When the identified killers were acquitted she put together a private investigation. She lobbied government to open a public inquiry. Her tireless campaigning made her a target for far-right abuse, but it also made her son's murder an important stake in the sand for race relations in the UK. Finally, in 2012, nineteen years after Stephen's death, two of the original defendants were jailed for his murder and Doreen Lawrence became a national hero.

While there is no question Doreen Lawrence would give back everything she has achieved to have Stephen by her side, what his death did was allow her to unearth strength she would not ordinarily have found. The same is true of John Walsh, known to many as the presenter of *America's Most Wanted*. To millions he is the silver fox who dresses like the man from Milk Tray and signs off by saying: 'Remember, you can make a difference.' But what many do not know about Walsh is that he not only created the highly successful TV series, but that he and his wife have been instrumental in creating both the Missing Children Act of 1982 and the Missing Children's Assistance Act of 1984. (And if you've ever seen a milk carton in the US with a picture of a missing child on the back – that too was Walsh's initiative.)

Walsh has also known trauma. On 27 July 1981 Walsh's seven-year-old son, Adam, was abducted from a Sears department store in Florida. Sixteen days later his severed head was found in a drainage canal, 120 miles from where he lived. Again, here was a man who suffered unimaginable loss, compounded by the fact that Walsh and his wife never knew for sure who the killer was until twenty-six years later, when serial killer Ottis Toole was charged with the murder. And yet, Walsh went on to become one of America's leading victim-rights advocates.

PROCESSING MAJOR DISCOMFORT

Trauma, if not dealt with, can hang over you for the rest of your life, often in unconscious ways. Ever noticed how you can tell which kids were bullied at school? They are often the ones who walk with a slight sag to their shoulders. They are awkward with eye contact. They tend to shy away from confrontation, preferring to stick to the edges of a situation.

And where does that get them? It makes them prey to further bullying. Human beings are very clever at picking up on unconscious signals. And untreated trauma can manifest itself in ways you didn't even realise.

So what should you do? Well, you start to pick through what went wrong. Let's take my example:

QUESTION 1: How had I got to a place where I was being forced out of my dream job because I'd overlooked a pile of admin?
A: Well, maybe it wasn't just about the admin. Maybe I was letting things get out of control in other parts of the job too.

QUESTION 2: Why would you let that happen?
A: I did it because I struggle with organisation, but had said I was organised in my job interview.

QUESTION 3: Why do you struggle with organisation?
A: I struggle because I'm not naturally organised, but am also afraid of asking for help for fear of looking weak and under-qualified for my job.

QUESTION 4: Why did no one notice sooner that you were out of your depth though?
A: Because I never communicated properly with my team.

QUESTION 5: Why didn't you communicate with them?
A: I was scared of getting negative feedback on anything.

Journaling is a great way of rinsing a painful experience of its discomfort and, thankfully, that was what I did. However, through the line of questioning I've just demonstrated, I could have got to the crux of the issue much sooner. The problem (at least the ones within my control) were two-fold. Basically, I didn't like communicating because I was scared of getting feedback I might not have liked the sound of. Interestingly, as a boss I'm now obsessional about feedback and communication. I get nervous if anyone goes quiet on a project and force many of my long-suffering team to comb back through something that went wrong. That way, we have a framework so that it (hopefully) never happens again. And if it does? Then we'll know how to deal with it.

Did it work? Well, to cut a long story short, I stayed in that job for a further sixteen months. And by the time they threw me a great big leaving party, I was devastated to be going. I can honestly say it was one of the most career-defining jobs I have ever had. And the most influential part of it? That meeting with my editor, because that excruciating moment, and the discomfort I forced myself into afterwards by examining what had gone wrong, was the beginning of my true growth within the workplace.

HOW TO BUILD YOURSELF BACK UP AFTER TRAUMA

In the scheme of things, getting a serious ticking off by your editor isn't that big a deal. You may have to confront far greater things in your life. The point is, you can use the same methodology to work through whatever it is you are facing.

Psychotherapists and psychologists call this 'exposure therapy'. It is one of the most recognised procedures for dealing with something that frightens you: forcing yourself to come face to face with it. This doesn't make the experience in and of itself any less difficult (the loss of a job or a partner is always going to be something most of us would rather avoid), but the habitual exposure to it does make it easier to deal with over time.

It's horrible having to confront the very thing that terrified you, because you feel as if you're going to have to relive it all over again. But that's kind of the point. And, in the immediate term, you may experience the fear more acutely. That's okay – and part of the process.

Here's how you make it easier and less scary: dissect it. Pull the experience apart like a jigsaw, and then examine every piece in detail. Human nature finds it much easier to process things when they scale them back. I don't know about you, but when I'm going on a long run, I don't think about the ten kilometres I have to run. I think about each small landmark I have to get to along the way. And the more I do that, the more the run becomes less painful and more enjoyable, until, after a relatively short amount of time I can do the entire thing without even thinking about it. It's kind of like having stabilisers on your bike. Most of us have those things attached to our bicycles for far longer than we actually need them. But you keep them while your psychophysiological make-up is getting used to the sensation of riding a bike.

In the same way that Sajda started to pick apart what had led to the events of 7/7, the more you analyse your situation, the more your understanding will grow in terms of how to deal with it, should it ever happen again. And that's reassuring for your brain, because not having a template of how to deal with a repeat of this sort of event causes you to panic. Your brain fills with anxiety. You don't know how to behave. And nine times out of ten you'll walk right back into the same traumatic hole.

Like Sajda said, you have to get back on the train, so to speak, to get to the place you need to go. Here's how you do just that.

THE JIGSAW METHOD

The following method is based on the practices of exposure therapy, but with a few extra guidelines that I've found work for me, and those I have led, in my career. You can do this practice mentally (when you're walking to work in the morning, say) or you can do it with an obliging friend. I tend to prefer writing it down. That's a personal choice, largely because I'm a writer, but also because I find it can be helpful to read back through how you made sense of a difficult situation should you ever need to fall back on it.

1. **Take fifteen minutes to start:** I tend to think anything less than this and you're not giving yourself enough time to fully explore the situation. It could be a fifteen-minute walk, or fifteen minutes sat in silence or with your diary open and your pen poised. Go through what happened, adding as much detail as you can. Set the alarm on your clock. Fifteen minutes

will feel like a long time, but if you're going through it in enough detail, really mentally throwing yourself back in, then you may need even longer.

2. **Start with 'how?':** Once you've worked your way through the series of events and have them in some sort of coherent order then you need to delve in. The aim here is to go as far back as you can. That will be hard at first. Let's use the example of someone getting fired. How did this happen? Well, it happened because I was late for work every day and I didn't respect my boss. Okay, so how come you were late for work every day? The answer might be because you overslept. So then ask yourself, how is it that you overslept when you knew you had work the next day? Well, maybe you went to bed too late. Right, but how did that happen when you knew you had to be up early? Well, because I didn't really care if I was a bit late for work every day. You keep picking and picking at the problem until you get to the core. This won't happen overnight, by the way. A friend who can push you will really help here, because I often find most of us stop too early in this process. If you don't have someone to do this, then try asking 'how?' seven times. This should get you far enough into the problem to be able to start gnawing at the roots of it.

3. **Follow with 'why?':** Once you've hit upon the reason, you need to question why you behaved like this. In this example, you would need to look at why it is that you didn't care if your boss saw you coming in late every day. Is it that you felt better than your boss.

If so, why? Is it that you wanted to draw attention to yourself? Well, let's explore why that is then. Is it that you felt overqualified for the job and so believed coming in late didn't really make any difference to your performance? The essential thing to remember here is that you cannot blame the other person. Remember what I said about only working with what you can control? You couldn't control the way your boss behaved at work, only how *you* behaved. So, if the answer you come up with is: 'I behaved this way because my boss is a moron', then you need to restart, taking the emphasis away from the other person. You can't change your boss, but you can change your behaviour to be better equipped to deal with them.

4. **Chase up with 'what?':** Say the reason you came in late is because you felt a bit 'over' the job. It didn't feel like a challenge anymore and you were just going through the motions. What could you have done to change that? Could you have put time in with your boss to ask for extra responsibilities to extend your role? Could you have applied yourself to your own personal project every morning before work to get you out of bed? Keep asking until you come up with at least three or four options that you can work with. Organise them in order of preference and then start to make them happen.

By working through this checklist every time you go through personal trauma, you will become stronger and more adept at dealing with uncomfortable situations when they arise.

4

THE CURSE OF SOCIAL PERFECTIONISM

Letting go of what people think

Have you ever noticed how you can perform a speech with all the confidence of a seasoned TED speaker when you're alone? How about the eloquence with which you can talk about yourself and your accomplishments when it's just you and a mirror for company? Ever wondered why you can perform a perfect headstand when there's no one to witness it? Or recount a joke with the perfectly nuanced timing and deadpan delivery of Sarah Silverman when there's, ironically, no one to laugh at it?

If you've ever given any thought to even one of the above, I'll tell you why: other people's opinions – of you. Or, more accurately, what you *think* other people's opinions are of you. The reason we find ourselves freezing in the middle of a speech is not because we don't know the lines, but because we've suddenly seen someone in the audience whose opinion we value and fear their judgement. Not being able to recount every high-achieving detail of your life in the middle of an interview situation is not due to a failure to recall them, but because you are paralysed by the discomfort of what the person in front of you thinks. Once you add people to the mix, you also add a huge weight of *perceived* discomfort to the situation. It is a sort of the internal agony we all feel of being judged. And, trust me, *everyone* suffers from it.

THE CURSE OF THE SOCIAL PERFECTIONIST

For most of my life I have been a social perfectionist. That is to say, I care deeply about what other people think of me. This has tripped me up at all stages of my life, both personally and professionally. There have been men in my life that I have fallen hopelessly in love with and who will never know it, because I was too scared to tell them for fear they would think I was foolish or pushy. There have been job opportunities I have never pushed for, not because I didn't feel ready for those jobs, but because I feared the judgement of the person on the other side of the interview table thinking: 'Who is this woefully out-of-her depth candidate?' And every time I see friends or colleagues perform karaoke I long to join in, but don't for fear of what they'll think of me. (I know, thirty-nine years old and I still care.)

Does any of this ring true for you? I bet it does. That's because most of us are, to some degree, social perfectionists. That is to say, we not only care about what others think about us, but what they *expect* from us. And that can lead to crippling internal discomfort, much of it often without validation. If you are a mother, for example, you worry that others expect you to fulfil the role of dutiful, attentive mother. If you are a leader, you worry that others expect you to fulfil the role of fearless warrior, ready at a moment's notice to lead your brigade through even the most uncomfortable patch. If you are a shop assistant, you worry that the manager expects you to be unfailingly polite, or if you're a father you worry that your family expects you to provide for them at all times. These are tough roles to consistently fulfil and, for those of us who measure high on the social perfectionist scale (we all fall somewhere along that scale), you cannot help but feel duty-bound to perform these roles and play up to these identities. And that can be dangerous. (Cataclysmic in some cases, with studies showing a direct correlation between those who are extreme social perfectionists and suicide rates.) When social perfectionists feel they have failed others, they feel utterly defeated, which is the reason many of us don't put ourselves out there to begin with. We are, we believe, setting ourselves up to let others down – and, in doing so, are setting ourselves up to let down ourselves.

But there is something we are forgetting: nobody cares. Not really. Certainly, not as much as we think. In fact, studies show that we all massively overestimate other people's opinions of us. The truth is, most people are too busy thinking about themselves to think about you. I have come to this conclusion when I give speeches. A lot of my internal discomfort comes from worrying about what the audience will think of the way I move my hands or the way I walk across the stage. Yet, the more I look at the audience, the more I realise they are not thinking about me at all. I know this because every time I listen to a speech (and in general I'm pretty attentive) I barely give the speaker a second thought. Yes, I vaguely listen to what they are saying. And, yes, they will have made a vague impression on me when they walked onto the stage, but by the time they're even a few minutes into their speech? My eyes are wandering, or I'm thinking about what they're saying in relation to myself and my life.

Psychologists call this the 'spotlight effect' – the phenomenon of thinking people notice more about us than they actually do. There's a funny meme that sums this up perfectly. It shows a woman with bad-ish hair. And her thought bubble reads: 'When the fear is not really about having a bad hair day, but about people noticing it!' But imagine what you would do and what you could achieve if you thought other people weren't judging you. You'd probably speak up more in group situations (I used to speak up far less than I do now, not because I wasn't sure I was right, but because of my internal discomfort of what I thought everyone else in the group would think). You'd probably wear brighter clothes. You'd probably put yourself forward for jobs you suspected others thought were outside your league and capabilities, and you'd probably ask out a hell of a lot more potential partners if you carried less judgement about their supposed judgement of you. If this is you, you're not alone by the way. Some of our most impressive public figures feel the same. Actress Kristen Stewart has said: 'I care deeply what people think. I'm an actor: all I care about is being understood. All I want to do is convey myself.' *All* of us are plagued by the discomfort of what we think others think of us.

THE CONFORM NORM

But why? *Why* do we care so much? Well, we care so much because the desire to be liked is an integral part of being human. It's a feeling as primitive as the apes', designed in fact to keep us alive. Think about it: don't you love it when people agree with you. Have you ever noticed how you'll direct your conversation to the person in the group who nods when you talk? Or the way in which bosses tend to favour those colleagues who parrot their own views? Or how about the way in which Instagram has rapidly overtaken Twitter in popularity? Instagram being an egomaniacal echo chamber of likes and sycophantic commentary; Twitter being a public repository for name-calling and dissenting viewpoints.

It's in our biological make-up. We literally cannot help it. Getting along with our 'tribe' ensured that we stayed within it. And when you're living in harsh conditions where food is scarce, as our ancestors were, the group that stays together is the group that survives together. Nowhere is this more pronounced than in reality television. *Big Brother*, *Shipwrecked*, *The Colony*, *I'm a Celebrity Get Me Out of Here* – all work on the same basic human premise: do everything you can to stay within the group. Even if that means shielding a true part of who you are.

Don't just take it from me either. In an experiment undertaken by the University of California (UCLA), scientists tracked a group of teenagers' brains to see what happened when pictures they had posted on a social network site were liked by others. The result? When the teens saw their images had received a large number of likes, the part of their brain associated with 'reward' (in other words, the bit that registers pleasure) lit up like a fairground.

But what's even more interesting than that was that those same teens were more likely to 'like' an image if it had already received a large number of 'likes' from their peers. Coincidence? Or the purest form of expression to show exactly what we're talking about. We care what others think about us to such a degree that we let our opinion of what we think they think dictate the direction of our decisions.

But what is it that we're so afraid of? After all, we no longer have to stay within our social groups in order to survive. (Though numerous studies do show that those ostracised by their social group can experience depression and anxiety.) If we disagree with or disappoint those around us, what is the worst that can happen? If we give a speech that goes slightly off-track, we may irritate a few in the crowd. No biggie. If we tell an off-colour joke at the office party then we may lose favour with a few co-workers. So be it . . . But it's not that. Not really. What we're fighting for in today's world is not physical survival. It's social survival. And that can be a minefield of discomfort.

THE SOCIAL SELF

In the Western world we prize successful individuals with high social status. That doesn't mean we value those who have a big house or drive a fancy car more than we do someone who lives in a bedsit, but it does mean we are more attracted to those people who command respect within their social groups. In fact, researchers have found that high social status amongst our social group makes us happier than earning more money. (A study which backs this up, and one I have always found pretty amusing, is the one that discovered most people would rather earn £50,000 if all their friends were earning £25,000, than earn £250,000 when all their friends are earning £1 million.)

What is high social status, exactly, if it's not about money? It's about positioning. An individual with high social status is the person in your group whom others defer to. It is the person who others, often unconsciously, emulate. You'll have seen this in action when colleagues suddenly start dressing or talking in a similar way to their managers. Psychologists call this a 'prestige cue' – the act of deferring to and copying the person in the group who has the most attention. A large part of high social status is having your viewpoint held in high regard by your group. Ever wondered who has the highest social status in your group? A good litmus test to find out is to start a debate and see whose opinion everyone else starts to come around to. You may be surprised who it actually is.

So, if having high social status is what we all crave, then losing it, or having low social status, is what we want to avoid. At all costs. And that, therefore, is what we think is at risk when performing in front of others. And make no mistake, social status can be lost quickly and mercilessly. The one-time British Labour Party leader Ed Miliband found this out when he was caught, just days before local elections, eating a bacon sandwich. No major crisis, you may think. But the poor man was photographed mid-bite, with butter oozing out of his mouth and his eyes half-closed. It became front-page news a year later during the General Election campaign of 2015, when the *Sun* newspaper featured the photograph with the headline: 'This is the pig's ear Ed made of a helpless sarnie. In 48 hours he could be doing the same to Britain. SAVE OUR BACON.'

Debate spread like wildfire across social media and the British press as to whether his inability to eat a sandwich was indicative of his ability to perform as future leader of the country. Memes of him eating, his eyes rolling to the back of his head as he chewed a mouthful of bread, littered social feeds across the world with the hashtag #EdEats. Labour lost the election, Miliband stepped down and his political career was over. He had been made a laughing stock and, in the process, had lost his social status. And once he had lost his social status it was almost impossible for him to lead anyone any more.

So you see, the loss of social status can be quick and it can be devastating. But the internal discomfort of fearing we *may* lose social status is of far greater danger to us, because it stops us from taking on those very things we need to in order to move forward with our lives.

DOUBLE UP YOUR EFFORTS

It's all well and good telling ourselves that no one really cares about us, but how much less do they care about us than we think? About 50 per cent less according to studies. That's a lot. It means people are taking in only half of what you think they are. That almost certainly means that they are not picking up on marks on your top, day-old hair, and the way you move your hands just so when you're talking. Nope. None of that. Just knowing that is liberating, isn't it?

So, if people only notice roughly half of what you're doing, that means that if you really want them to take note (and by the end of this book we will be in the business of wanting people to take notice of us – just not with any of the neurosis we usually attach to it) then you can turn the volume up on all sorts of different behaviours.

If you're giving a speech, you can open your arms to their full width, rather than just half their width as most people do (and you'll notice that most great orators do this). It means you can speak twice as loudly in a room without anyone thinking it was out of the ordinary, or leave a pause of twice the length when adding dramatic emphasis to a talk. I call this 'doubling up' and you should do it whenever you can, without fear that anybody will judge you for it. Will they notice you? Yes. But they will notice you because you are performing to just the right level, not because you are making a fool of yourself.

Go ahead, try it. I suggest making a small film of yourself giving a short speech. Make sure you have someone in the room – a friend or an obliging partner will do. In the first take, talk as you would normally talk. In the second, be conscious of 'doubling up' on everything. Maybe you walk twice as far when you're speaking. After all, have you ever noticed how most professional speakers walk a *really* long way across a stage and we don't think it's strange at all? Next, try opening your arms twice as far as you normally would. It will feel a little odd, I know. But go with it. When you want to emphasise a word, speak it twice as loud as you normally would. It may feel like you're shouting, but you aren't. Have faith. And the pauses ... oh the pauses. This is the bit most speakers get wrong. It feels too daunting to leave a silence in the middle of a speech, doesn't it? But try to wait twice as long as you would naturally before you begin to talk. It may feel like a silence that stretches out for minutes, but in actual fact it will only be around a few seconds. Feel that silence. Get comfortable with the discomfort of it.

When you're performing both speeches they will feel very different. The first will feel comfortable, while the other will make you feel like you're taking part in some weird improv sketch. But it only feels that way because you're worried about making an enormous fruit gum out of yourself. Now watch the videos back. Notice how there is only a very subtle difference between the two? Except that one is much more compelling, much slicker and certainly much more impactful than the other. To the average person who only notices 50 per cent *less* of what you think they notice, they will only see a brilliant, accomplished speaker.

OPEN UP YOUR FEARS

Our fears of others' opinions are actually a projection of our own fears. Say someone says to you: 'You've got horrible green hair', you'd know not to take any notice, because in your mind you'd know that it isn't true. (Well, unless that DIY highlighting kit went horribly wrong.) But if someone says to you: 'You know, you didn't speak with any authority during that interview', then you'd believe them, because it echoes your own private negative beliefs about yourself.

A lot of people would give you the following advice: 'Stop believing the negative, self-sabotaging talk.' But this isn't that kind of book, and I'm not that sort of person. If life was that easy we'd all be shrugging off everything, letting thoughts of: 'Do I look fat in this? Do I gesticulate too much? Do I smell after having used that crystal non-deodorant deodorant?' slide off us like butter on hot toast. And we don't, because it's really hard to do.

Instead, here's what I say: own the discomfort of what you imagine others think of you by putting yourself out there. Accept that you'll feel a certain way – scared of what your boss will think of you before a meeting, nervous of what a new date will think of you, twitchy before a speech because of the 'judgemental' audience, whatever . . . and admit it to others. By releasing those feelings of internal discomfort, you also release yourself from the shame attached to them.

This will feel like being freed from an iron grasp, one created by you. When you release a thought or a feeling that you have kept boxed up inside you for weeks, months – in some people's cases, years – you are allowing yourself to no longer be internally defined by it. I mean . . . why do you think Catholics have confessionals?

Of course, I'm not saying the end goal is to release yourself from shame and internal discomfort altogether, which can be simultaneously positive and negative. Both can sometimes be useful in telling us when we have behaved inappropriately, and you should use that and listen to it. But any emotion taken to an extreme is destructive. And shame without merit, shame that we have imposed on ourselves because of fear of what others think, can be extreme. It also means we can end up with ideas about who we are that actually have zero basis in who or what we actually are.

Start by talking to someone you trust – a close friend, your partner, or a work colleague you have known for years and with whom you feel safe. Or just grab the person you did the DIY video with. (I'd put them on some sort of commission by the end of this book, actually, because you're going to be calling on them a lot.) Tell them how you're feeling. If it's before a big meeting, tell them you're feeling 'nervous' about the opinion of others in the room. And go into detail: explain exactly what it is that you're nervous about, because chances are it won't be the entire situation, just an element of it. So maybe you're anxious about what will happen if you're asked to give your opinion and don't have an answer. What will they think of you? Will they think you're stupid? Not qualified for the job? Or maybe you're nervous about making your voice heard over the other strong characters in the room. By admitting your internal discomfort, you will discover four things that you probably didn't know before:

1. Everyone feels the same. And simply knowing this will automatically make you feel better.
2. The person you're confiding in will be surprised, since what you're feeling inside is rarely what anybody else thinks. I've lost count of the number of times I've told someone I'm feeling nervous and they've turned around and said: 'But you'd never know.' That is also guaranteed to make you feel better. Trust me.

3. It will release you from feeling defined by that feeling. According to studies, internalising any discomfort or negative emotion is not only detrimental to our health (those that keep things bottled up are at a greater risk of suffering from heart disease), but also put us at risk of clouding our judgement about who we really are.

4. It will make you feel brave. Simple as. And feeling proud of being brave is a great motivator and something a lot of people don't often feel in their life.

I want to just settle on point four for a minute, because feeling brave is a highly undervalued, yet essential, element to human consciousness. When you feel brave, when you're in that mindset, you feel you can take on the world. When you're in that headspace you really don't give a damn what anyone else thinks.

Acknowledging your own internal discomfort is about one of the bravest things you can do, and yet so few of us allow ourselves to do it. Why? Because we fear our loss of status by admitting our perceived weaknesses. But as we've seen in this chapter, people rarely take as much notice as we think they do, so what have you got to lose by admitting to being scared? Nothing. What, on the other hand, have you got to gain? Everything.

The truth is most people are scared, but those who insist they aren't are either A: naïve (and that's when things can really go wrong) or B: narcissists (also with the potential for a lot to go wrong in their lives). Naïve people don't have a grip on the situation at hand. If they think they won't be scared walking out onto a stage in front of five hundred people, or entering a tricky interview situation, then the minute fear hits them they will be floored. Finished. That's when you'll see the 'discomfort paralysis', which we've already talked about, and they'll have nothing to fall back on. It's a bad look for both the audience and the naïve person who put themselves out there. Plus, once that happens, the internal discomfort you felt about everyone judging you for being a bad performer becomes true!

No, the smart person admits they're scared – ideally, to another person. And they break down exactly what their internal discomfort is made of. This is how exposure therapy works. You expose yourself to the very thing you are afraid of, as often as possible. Clinical literature shows that, in doing so, people don't get just less afraid, they get *braver*. The crux is this, however: they only become braver if the exposure is *voluntary*. If it's involuntary then the opposite can happen. So, if you're scared of what other people are going to think of you, you admit it. Put it out there. Stand up to it before anyone has a chance to lay it on you. The difference between saying, 'I am scared of doing a talk in front of five hundred people' and someone saying to *you*, 'You are scared of doing this talk in front of five hundred people, aren't you?' is immense.

When you voluntarily expose yourself to something you are afraid of (in this case, the judgement of others) you go into a 'challenge state'; and a challenge state, as we've discussed, elicits positive emotions.

There's another wonderful and unexpected side effect to owning your internal discomfort: people love it. They admire it. They recognise the bravery and the ownership of that fear, and it resonates with how they would like to lead their own lives.

An example: in 1991, the late George Michael appeared on *Parkinson*, at the time one of the most widely watched talk shows in the UK. Some months previously George Michael had been found in a Beverly Hills public toilet soliciting for sex. It was front-page news for weeks. First, because no one had known George Michael was gay. And secondly, because of the way in which he was found out. (Although, by Michael's own admission, if you're going to do it in a public toilet, you may as well do it in a Beverly Hills public toilet. I have stayed in the hotel directly in front of said toilets and they really are knockout for a public loo.)

It was one of the first times that George Michael talked publicly about the incident – he'd refused to speak about it previously – and the world was waiting. Waiting and watching for him to perform twenty minutes of PR-approved guff. The singer knew everyone was marking time until Parkinson got over all the chit-chat about his music and career, and on to talking about what happened in the toilet that night. It must have been a source of huge internal discomfort for him. So, what did George Michael do? He owned his internal discomfort.

Before Parkinson had a chance to ask him, and relatively early on in the interview, George Michael brought up the scandal himself, making light of the fact that he would rather not have revealed to the world he was gay by being found in a public toilet. It was a magical moment: Parkinson appears visibly shocked, while George Michael looks, for the first time during the interview, comfortable. It would have been a very brief moment of discomfort for him, but, in putting himself through it, rather than waiting for Parkinson to do it, he controlled the situation. And in taking control of his own internal discomfort he didn't allow others to define or shame him. What's more, the world recognised his bravery in doing so.

George Michael, once again, became the nation's sweetheart and sales of his album soared by 70 per cent after the interview was broadcast. (Interestingly, Ed Miliband took a similar approach after 'Bacongate', sending out Christmas cards that featured him dressed as a slick, leather-clad biker eating a bacon sarnie. He totally owned the discomfort of the situation and everyone I know who got one of those cards loved him for it.)

Susan MacTavish Best knows all about owning internal discomfort. She is the Martha Stewart of Silicon Valley, a woman known for bringing together some of the most influential names from the worlds of tech, business, academia and arts under the roof of her San Francisco home. To be invited to a MacTavish Best 'salon' is to feel as though you've arrived. On any given evening you will find Nobel Prize-winners talking to award-winning writers; Hollywood film producers mingling with tech founders. And there, at the centre of it all, is Susan – a lithe, flame-haired presence whose job it is to move round the room, introducing and assuaging with all the deftness of a foreign diplomat, as well as to hold court amongst some of the most powerful people on the planet. To watch her in action is to watch someone so at ease with herself and the judgement of others that you wonder what her secret is. The answer was a brief moment of life-changing discomfort that could have ended her entire career.

On 25 January 2002, as she cleared away the vestiges from yet another late-night salon, Susan leaned over the fire that still smouldered in the front room and BAM! Flames leapt towards her face and started to engulf her body.

'It felt like I had cotton candy all over my cheeks,' she tells me, 'but as I moved my hands towards my face to pat it away I realised my whole face was on fire.' The next few minutes passed in a blur. She remembers jumping in the shower, running around the room to make sure nothing else was alight and then finally hearing the ambulance sirens approach.

For the first few weeks it was touch and go whether she would even live. She lay in hospital, a human rag doll, her limbs suspended around her. When doctors finally told her she had come through the worst, she then had to come to terms with the lasting damage to her body. She had suffered second- and third-degree burns to 20 per cent of her body. Her legs, arms, hands and face were affected the worst. Only a pair of glasses she had been wearing that night saved her eyesight. She was too sick to look in a mirror, but she could feel the damage. Her entire face, from forehead to chin, felt like the surface of the moon, mounds of open suppurating blisters covering her once-beautiful porcelain skin. It would be a miracle if she ever looked the same again.

And yet ... when she was released from hospital several weeks later she had a decision to make. Would she hide away from the social scene she had been such an instrumental cog in because of her own internal discomfort of what she believed others would think of her transformed appearance? Or would she face the stares and whispers she was so scared of?

In the end, she confronted them. 'I wanted to feel that life was moving forwards. So, just a few weeks later, I threw a big salon, cooking for people with one leg up on the kitchen counter (I had to keep it up at all times!). Sure, I was slightly jarred when a few people said how brave I was for letting others see me in that way, but, ultimately, I didn't care how others saw me. Most people barely commented at all.'

LEARNING TO LET GO OF INTERNAL DISCOMFORT

Finally, the only way to *truly* not care what others think about you is to have a solid sense of who you are. Easier said than done, I know. But often, we don't ever find out who we really are or what we really think because, unconsciously, we are afraid of being excluded. That means some people can spend their entire lives not knowing what really makes them tick – and that's a sad place to be. In order not to be excluded we repeat phrases and opinions we have heard before. So much so that pretty soon we don't know where we start and everyone else begins.

Well, here's where you start. You start by saying phrases you think apply to you. Maybe that word is frightened. Maybe that word is creative. As you're saying each word, pay attention to how you feel when you say it. Does it make you feel stronger or weaker? If it makes you feel weaker, then don't say it anymore. Instead, keep saying the word that makes you feel strong.

Part of the key to nuking your internal discomfort about what the world thinks about you is to remember that most people don't have an opinion about us, full stop. Simply knowing and reminding yourself of that is incredibly liberating. But also, and I think this is crucial, if you still can't get those nig-gling thoughts out of your head, then confide in someone you trust. A trusted friend who has the ability to be as impartial as they are caring can help you navigate your internal discomfort. They can tell you whether your fear is founded on something true or is simply a projection of your own fears – and often you'll find it is the latter. As author Olin Miller once said, 'You probably wouldn't worry about what people think of you, if you could know how seldom they do.'

5

UNEXPECTED DISCOMFORT

. . . and how your gut instinct can save you

A couple of years ago I was asked to interview a tech founder at a conference. I had been told little about the conference other than that I had thirty minutes on stage at the end of the day. But when I arrived both myself and the chap in question realised we were speaking in the biggest arena in the entire country – in front of 20,000 people. The largest number of people I had ever spoken in front of was fifty. The tech guy looked at me and I looked back at the tech guy and we both kind of giggled in the manner of two children who realise something really bad is about to happen. We were stranded in our discomfort zone without a buoy and no idea how to stop ourselves from sinking.

'Okay . . . so it's a *massive* crowd out there!' yelled the show's completely over-adrenalised organiser to us backstage. 'They're all *hyped*! This is the final act! I want you to go out there and be *rock stars*.'

The man I was about to interview, though charming to a fault, was not a rock star. He was a tech wizard in pressed shirt and jeans. I was a middle-aged journalist in a tuxedo. We were about as far from rock stars as it's possible to get. Then, as the countdown began (60 seconds ... 45 seconds ... 30 seconds ...), he delivered his final uterus-twitching coup de grâce: 'Oh and we have to get some pictures, so we'll need you both to stand in front of the crowd for fifteen seconds while we get those.' Before we knew it our names were announced and we were cast out into the blinking light. I imagine if you're a genuine rock star – a Mick Jagger or a Beyoncé, say – then the feeling of having all those smiling faces pointed in your direction is exhilarating. Everyone is there because they want to see you. But no one was smiling when we stepped out. They just waited there, expectantly. Frowning.

I had no idea what to do, who to look at or how to keep the crowd engaged. I waited for rational thought to kick in and give me an answer, but it didn't come. What felt like whole minutes ticked by as the discomfort engulfed me. I started to perspire under the white arena lights. My body felt stiff, like it had just come out of the deep freeze, even though it was thirty degrees in there. Come on, come on, I willed myself. What do I do? *What do I—*'

And then something miraculous happened. My gut kicked in and, for the first time in years, I listened to it. Before I knew it, I was instructing the heaving crowd of men and women to raise their phones to the sky, turn their lights on and have a giant selfie with me and my guest. And the craziest thing: not only did they oblige, but they hung like that for the fifteen seconds it took for me and my guest to fiddle with our phones in order to capture the scene. The hysterical organiser got his picture; my interviewee felt calm and relaxed before our talk; and I didn't defecate in front of an arena of thousands. It was a good moment. When you find yourself mired in a discomfort zone that feels wildly out of control, the buoy you need to lift you to safety is your gut.

WHY YOUR GUT IS A SILENT HERO

If had waited for the fractional few seconds for rational thought to kick in when I was standing up there, then I have no doubt my body would have given way. I would have been consumed by 'discomfort paralysis' as I waited for my thoughts to click into place. My body would have frozen and it would have been game over. Instead my gut had the answer. And saved the moment.

But what is gut instinct but a bunch of emotions, right? A hunch. A feeling. Sure, it's all of those things, but it is also one of your body's most useful tools. Gut instinct is what firefighters, pilots, the police and the armed forces turn to time and again when they find themselves in their discomfort zone. In fact, studies compiled by Gary Klein, one of the world's leading thinkers on intuition and gut instinct, found that army officers used gut instinct in 96 per cent of their decision-making, while naval commanders used it in 95 per cent of theirs.

This is because, in times of intense discomfort – those pressurised moments when time is not on your side and your body's burning up stress like dead wood in a forest fire – rational thought often doesn't have time to kick in. Wait for it to come and instead your anxiety will build. And build. And as your anxiety rises your thoughts – those rational, smart thoughts you're hoping will save you – will get muddled. You will become even more anxious and, before you know it, you're in full-on panic mode – and then in 'discomfort paralysis' hell.

Why is your gut better at rescuing you during brief moments of intense discomfort than your rational thoughts? It's because your body often recognises discomfort way before you do. I'll give you an example: logging into your bank account. It's a simple enough action and yet it's suffused with fear. We all hold our breath and feel the slow creep of dread as the numbers start to download on the screen. We get a little dry-mouthed. Sometimes we even feel a bit sick. This is crazy, rational thought tells you. Why am I feeling this way? It's just a screen with some numbers printed on it! But it isn't really. And your body knows this. It understands that those are not just numbers on the screen: they represent your current life and your future life. They are an accurate window into how you behave in the real world – all the times you spent money you didn't have; when you threw responsibility to the wind; when you acted impulsively and without thought. It is a list of numbers that acknowledges who you really are. And that is uncomfortable.

And that's why you can't always trust rational thought. It's open to manipulation. It can restructure narrative at will. It can sell you the story you want to hear rather than the one you need to hear. Your body on the other hand? There's no way to manipulate a stress response. No way to re-spin a rapidly beating heart. No way to disguise sweating palms and a perspiring upper lip.

Not only can your gut act far quicker than your brain, but it's a truth teller. Your gut can pick up on the slightest visual cues in nanoseconds. Your brain takes longer. Think about it. Have you ever been on a dark street at night and seen someone loitering on the street just ahead of you? My bet is you crossed the road before you had time to think about why. Once you rationalised why you did this you will probably have told yourself one of the following:

He was a lone man out at night. That's never a good sign.

He was looking in my direction. Probably sizing up my bag.

He was wearing a hooded top. Why would he be wearing a hooded top? *With the hood up!*

Of course, there may have been many reasons for all those behaviours. He might have been locked out of his house and had to hang about until his mum got back with the house keys. He may well have been looking at you, but maybe to see if he knew you – after all, he knows most people in the area. And what about his hooded top? It's freezing. He's got cold ears. And besides, it's Alexander Wang. You're meant to *wear it with the hood up!*

Now you could have stopped and thought it through. You could have taken a really long hard look at the poor guy and then made a more informed decision, but it's late. And it's dark and, frankly, that would just be plain weird. Hell, *he'd* probably cross the road. So, you have one thing to go on: your gut. And your gut says: *Cross the road. Now!*

Gut instinct is a bit like those 'wise old women' Hollywood always gets Maggie Smith to play. It just *knows*. And in times of discomfort it knows best.

BAD STUFF HAPPENS TO YOUR BODY WHEN YOU DON'T LISTEN TO YOUR GUT

Have you ever been in a job interview when the interviewer has thrown you a curveball? Or maybe you've given a speech and someone has heckled you from the back? Rational thought doesn't kick in, does it? Or if it does, it isn't quick enough. In the time it takes for your mind to formulate a response a whole lot of weird physical reactions – facial tics, dilated pupils and clammy hands/forehead/underarms – have started to give the game away.

Pop 'Theresa May' and 'wheat fields' into YouTube and witness one of the most catastrophic leanings on rational thought in political history. In what should have been a relatively light-hearted interview, the presenter asks May to recall the naughtiest thing she has ever done. The Prime Minister's first instinct is to say: 'Oh goodness me!' before a mortifying physical disintegration happens right in front of the presenter's (and millions of viewers') eyes. May's mouth drops open, her shoulders slump, she looks away before her entire mouth crumples into the sort of hapless crinkle only ever seen on hand puppets. Never has there been a more cringe-inducing image of human discomfort. It is one of the worst moments of her political career and no one in Britain has ever been able to look at a field of wheat again without imagining a young Theresa May crushing the hell out of stalks while being chased by a farmer with an AK-47.

This is in stark contrast to Barack Obama, who, only a few years previously, was heckled by a voter in the White House.

Usually presidents are not allowed to contest voters. They are not even allowed to ask them to be removed (yes, even the most belligerent ones are only allowed to be removed if security make that call, not the president). But finally, exasperated (but still with a soft smile on his face), Obama said to the heckler: 'You're in my house now' – a polite but humorous call to sit down and shut the f**k up, the sort of thing you'd call on to tame a rowdy dinner guest. The audience tittered. Obama did not break sweat. (And in the end Obama completely broke with protocol and asked security to dispense with the man altogether.) This was pure instinct on Obama's part. No PR or Svengali would have instructed him to do this. Even though it went against every rule in the presidential book, it was somehow just right for that brief moment of discomfort.

So why are some people able to channel their gut, while others freeze and wait for rational thought to save them? A young firefighter from South Wales can tell you.

She knew only two things about the fire. First, that it was a house fire not far from the fire station and had been burning for some time. Second, that there were people trapped inside.

Sabrina Cohen-Hatton was only twenty-four, but she had already mountaineered her way up the ranks to become chief fire officer for the small station where she worked in South Wales. This meant it was her job, on her patch and she was in charge. As the other firefighters, all men much older than her, piled into the fire engine she climbed up in front.

'Okay everyone, it's a house fire, person's reported. We don't know how many people are in there and we don't know where they are.'

If they could blast through the traffic they'd be there in five minutes. Sabrina busied herself instructing the team. She had been in the job for almost six years now, but every time a new call came in her body responded in the same way – dry mouth, clammy hands and a racing heart that felt like a trapped butterfly deep inside her chest.

They pulled up outside the house, a narrow terrace typical in this part of Wales. Unlike the many house fires Sabrina had previously attended, there was something different about this one. It was quiet. Eerily so. There were no family members screaming for help or pointing to a bedroom window where a child had last been seen. There were no neighbours to brief her on the situation: how long it had been burning, who was in there, how many people lived at that address. Instead, she had nothing to go on but the fire itself: a thick, raging bloom that had already engulfed the entire building.

The call had said there were people inside. If they were in there they would almost certainly be trapped, gasping for air. And so Sabrina had a decision to make: send in her team to try and rescue those who were inside; or protect her own men, keep them back, contain the fire and live with the consequences. Seconds passed. Rational thought did not have time to make that call. Instead, standing there, deep in her discomfort zone – her men waiting for her command, breathing apparatus on – she had to make a decision. And that decision had to come from her gut.

'In the end I decided not to send my men in,' she tells me, a pretty, petite woman with the handshake of a WWF wrestler. 'It was a severe fire. There was smoke from the downstairs windows and the upstairs windows. For the upstairs to have caught fire that meant it had probably been burning for around thirty minutes at least. To be that advanced there would be little chance anyone in there would still be alive.' That meant to send her men in would be to risk their lives too. It was the right decision.

'Thankfully it turned out that there was no one inside. But we didn't know that at the time,' she tells me, as she sits on a small plastic seat inside the London Fire Brigade's central London office where she is now deputy assistant fire commissioner for the capital. (Sabrina was one of the fire chiefs who was sent down to Grenfell Tower in London's Notting Hill in the early hours of 14 June 2017 to attend to one of the most devastating and controversial fires in British history.)

The speed of our gut reaction is quick. That's why people like Sabrina, who work in high-pressure environments where timing is everything, are taught to rely on their gut. So how quick, exactly? Scientists have found it takes a tenth of a second for your instinct to respond to stimuli. That means you can have made a decision before you are even conscious of what your brain has registered. And sometimes, in discomfort zones when time is short, that's exactly what you need.

In a study on snap decision-making, subjects who were given a fraction of a second to produce an answer to a visual problem were correct 95 per cent of the time, while those who were given longer were right only 70 per cent of the time. Pure luck? Not exactly. It was found that those who took longer to make their decision had had their judgement clouded by too much information. It's kind of like when you go into Starbucks imaging you're going to walk away with an extra-hot skinny latte. But when you get there and look up at the board – which, since you last went in has gained an extra seventy-nine coffee options – you get 'Starbucks paralysis'. Literally. You stand there, unable to make this life-or-death decision, while the barista stares at you, Sharpie poised, and the guy behind you starts deep breathing into your earhole.

If gut instinct's right most of the time, then why are we so sceptical? Why do we put it up there with dreams and other woowoo? I've seen eyes roll and smirks spread across faces when colleagues have suggested their decisions have been based on raw gut. But we are wrong to judge this, because your brain is distributed throughout your entire body. In fact, there are more neurons in your autonomic system (basically your unconscious nervous system, which has the job of regulating everything from how often your heart is beating to how often you get horny) than in your entire central nervous system. This goes some way to explaining why many people refer to the gut as the 'second brain'. (The phrase gut throws some people because it suggests it's only associated with this part of your body. While many of the hallmark sensations of instinct do manifest themselves in and around the stomach – butterflies, that horrible sea-sick feeling you get – it's more of an *entire* body instinct.)

But why are some people's gut instincts so right-on, when others are so far off? Can you hone your gut to make the right decisions, to be as sharp and as accurate as a darts player's aim? The answer to this question is 'yes'. And once you've mastered how, you can sail through the trickiest of discomfort zones.

*

Reread how Sabrina made her decision. Look back over how systematic her response was. Notice how *rational* it is. What felt and looked like a gut reaction was, in fact, backed up by a huge amount of knowledge about the situation – knowledge that she had built through repeated exposure to similar experiences. This is known as 'pattern recognition' and anyone can build theirs in order to make better gut decisions. In some parts of your life you may in fact already do this.

For example, if you are a vintage obsessive you are probably used to scrabbling around at car-boot sales and rummaging through charity shop rails. So much so that often you can walk into a shop and know within minutes whether there is anything decent to be found. It's a 'gut instinct'. Or at least you *think* it is. But, in fact, all those hours you've spent vintage prowling has given you the ability to 'thin-slice' any vintage situation. 'Thin-slicing' is basically your brain's ability to do a kind of supersonic audit of the situation at hand, and it often happens without your even being conscious of it. It's like a magic power that can size up a situation – and, nine times out of ten, it helps you make the right decision.

Now, I know what you're thinking: give me some of that thin-slicing mystical magic. And you'd be right to want some. Sabrina was able to thin-slice the entire situation in front of her when she turned up to that fire in South Wales. Without realising it, I was also able to thin-slice the arena situation. Why? Because both of us had had experience of similar situations before. (Admittedly mine had been with a much smaller audience.)

'There would certainly have been other incidences that would have fallen into my underpinning knowledge of that [particular situation] but none of it would have been conscious enough to come to the forefront,' Sabrina tells me. 'But almost certainly other incidents that I had been to, looking at decisions other people had made in those kind of situations, the tactics they used.'

For me, it was similar. While the largest number of people I had spoken in front of publicly before that moment was fifty, I had given countless other talks before that moment. Which means the adage 'practice makes perfect' is only a half-truth. Because that old saying suggests you have to do the same thing over and over again in order to become brilliant. But in my experience, and in Sabrina's experience and the experience of police chiefs and politicians and leaders of all different persuasions, you don't have to have been thrown into the exact same discomfort zone again and again in order to hone a killer gut instinct. You simply need to have experienced vaguely similar discomfort zones before.

'Someone once said to me, you can have twenty years' experience doing the same thing, or you can have one year of experience doing twenty different things,' says Sabrina. 'The more experiences you have and the more diverse those experiences, then the better your gut instinct will be.'

So how the hell does that work? Well, the human mind has a thing about looking for patterns. It can figure out that the same techniques you used for giving a speech in front of three strangers can then be re-employed when you turn up to do a speech in a stadium in front of 20,000 people.

It can figure out that the three repetitious notes you used to compose a funny little ditty for your partner's birthday can be used to write a song of staggering beauty. It can work out how to deal with a tricksy CEO by drawing on that time you had to have a tête-à-tête with that deranged manager of your local corner shop. It's smart like that. You've just got to give it something to work with.

In other words, you need to throw yourself into discomfort. Some of it can be major, some of it minor. The point is you need to experience it to help build a pattern for when things get really uncomfortable. Because it's while you're there that your brain is quietly building patterns to be used at a later date. And it's these patterns that sharpen your gut instinct. If that sounds scary, it's not. Because the really clever thing is that you can throw yourself into a load of low-level moments of discomfort that will ultimately help you to ace those moments of high-level discomfort.

Let's say your discomfort zone is speaking in front of strangers. Start small. Take any opportunity you can to talk in front of a new audience. It may mean giving the toast at your next in-law family Christmas get-together. It might mean giving a small leaving speech in front of three or four colleagues over lunch. It doesn't matter. Every nuance, every laugh, every boob you make will be processed and stored away, helping to hone your pattern-recognition antennae. Do it as often as you can and try and focus on the parts you find most difficult. Is it getting your audience's attention at the beginning? Is it what to do when your joke falls flat? Write it down, and the next time you do it focus on these points. Not only will you become more skilled, but your gut instinct for how to behave in these situations will build and build. And in turn you will be able to connect with it faster and with more confidence.

As for me, I'm already planning to go back and perform at the same arena next year. Except this year the organisers tell me it's for 60,000 people.

6

THE FEEDBACK FIRING LINE

Turning the discomfort of criticism into a turning point in your career

A few years ago I found myself at a hotel that advertised itself as having a run club. I had a few hours to while away, had demolished most of the breakfast bar and so, as I tend to do when guilt gets the better of me, I found myself signing up. But when I arrived a few hours later, I discovered it was just me and the running instructor. She was a young girl, no older than twenty, who was dressed from collarbone to ankle in immaculate Lycra and startling white trainers.

'Hi there!' she shouted, in the over-enthusiastic manner of someone trying desperately to compensate for the lack of any real clients with the volume of her own voice.

'So, it's just the two of us today,' she said with a pained rictus grin. 'We have two choices. We can either run round the island with the route I had planned for today's group, or . . .'

and her eyes lit up at this point, 'we can use the track down the way. I can look at your running technique and then we can go for a run!' She looked at me in the same hopeful way my dog does when I'm putting on my shoes.

Look at my running technique? Either you can run or you can't, surely? It's one of those things, a bit like curling your tongue into one of those horrific fleshy cigarillos some people demonstrate at parties. It's a knack you either have or you don't. Besides, I was a pretty good runner. I was 100-metre county champion at eleven. I'd been running since I was knee high. I kept my hands as flat and rigid as an ironing board when I ran, my knees high, my stride long and strong. I didn't need coaching on how to run. And yet, I felt bad. It occurred to me that I was probably her only customer of the entire season.

'OK,' I said. 'I guess you can look at my running style.' And so off we headed. She started by having me run up and down the track, making little notes every time I passed her. Sometimes she would frown, other times she would nod approvingly. It was all very odd, until, when I eventually stopped, breathless and sweat-soaked, she turned to me and told me the following:

1. My elbows reared out when I ran. They needed keeping much closer to my body.
2. Did I realise I looked at the ground, not at the space in front of me, when I was running?
3. Oh and I was a bit flat-footed – my feet dragged against the ground. That would make running much harder.

4. And one last thing . . . my knees bent inwards. Had I ever had any knee issues after running? (The answer was yes – for years!)

The list went on and on, my jaw slackening every time she added a new observation to the list. But here's the thing, as embarrassed as I was to hear that I'd basically been running like a free-range chicken for the last twenty-five years of my life, it was, she told me, all adjustable. 'In fact,' she said, leaning in conspiratorially, 'you'll see a difference by the end of this session.' And she was right. For the entire hour I ran in a totally different manner, mindful of everything she had told me I was doing wrong. I picked my feet up, was aware of my knees, looked straight ahead of me when I ran and kept my elbows so close to my body I feared mild chafing.

It was miraculous. I felt as if I had a whole new lightness in my feet. I had always been a sprinter, powering over short distances, but telling myself I could never do anything longer than ten kilometres. But after that session I started to run greater distances. Now I can run for miles and I no longer have searing knee pain. And to think, all this happened because I whiled away a dead hour taking feedback from a girl I felt sorry for.

WHY YOU SHOULD LOVE YOUR CRITICS

When you hear the word 'feedback' what do you think of? Do you have images of a stern-faced line manager, a piece of A4 paper separating the two of you on which your entire career is mapped out in clumsy HR/performance review speak? Or maybe you think of a twisted colleague who 'helpfully' volunteers 'feedback' on everything you're doing wrong at work. Rarely do we think of it as a positive, life-enhancing thing. And yet, feedback is one of the simplest and most transformational tools out there. But here's the thing: it's a bit like sex – it's only transformational if you're getting it from the right person at the right time.

When it comes to feedback we are a culture that cowers. We don't like giving it and we sure as hell don't like receiving it. Most of us were raised under a parental cloud of overpraise. Motivate kids, our parents were told! Lift them up! Make them roll through life on casters of confidence and high self-esteem by telling them only what they are good at. And if you do have to give real, critical feedback, temper it with at least three positive things. Sound familiar? Surely you've experienced this claptrap before? I know I have. I've received it and, for my sins, have tried to dole it out for years.

But here's another reason why we don't like feedback. Feedback reveals who we really are. Just like we saw with obstacles in Chapter Two, feedback offers you a direct portal to your weaknesses – and not everybody wants to take that journey. The truth is, most of us have spent a lifetime constructing a narrative of who we are. *I am ambitious. I am kind. I am brave.* And we go looking for signs and signals to confirm this about ourselves. And this is fine . . . if you plan on spending the rest of your life in complete isolation with no one to challenge that view. But if you want to get on and get ahead? You're going to have to step into the discomfort zone once again and learn how to take feedback.

*

In 2010, people across the world were eating terrible pizza. The crust was like cardboard, the sauce had the telltale vinegary tang of ketchup, while the cheese was so thick and plastic it may as well have been cooked up in a science lab. The name of the company doling out this substandard product? Domino's.

In March of that year, forty-seven-year-old Patrick Doyle was due to take over as CEO of the company. He had grown up with Domino's. Like most of us, he remembered the excitement of the teal-blue box arriving at his house, the ritualistic lifting of the lid to reveal a thick, steaming pizza dense with cheese, real tomato sauce and a soft pillowy crust. But by the time he took over the corner office the pizzas didn't look and taste quite like he'd remembered. And the company was suffering as a consequence. Sales were dropping, share prices were at an all-time low and they had come last in a consumer taste test of fast-food products.

Their problem? They had spent years going big on the delivery element of their pizza (Domino's invented pizza delivery in the 1960s), but along the way they had missed the whole point of the pizza business: the taste. This meant that, by 2008, Domino's had no fans, no loyalty to the brand and no option but to go back to basics and take a long, hard look at what they were doing.

Rather than sit around in a meeting room with their top executives, shooting the breeze on what to do, they decided to ask those who would give them the most crushing, critical feedback: their customers – the very same customers who were also ordering pizza from Papa John's, Little Caesars and Pizza Hut.

They set out across America to find dozens of lapsed Domino's fans, brought them into a room and made them eat pizza, filming their reactions throughout. The feedback was crushing. 'This tastes low quality and forgettable,' said one tester. 'Domino's crust is too rubbery,' said another. It went on. And on.

It was hard to hear. Doyle and his team knew the pizzas weren't up to much, but hadn't realised quite how off the mark they were. It didn't matter. With the words 'rubbery', 'cardboard' and 'low quality' ringing in their ears, they set to work completely reformulating their pizzas.

Now I know what you're thinking: so far so unremarkable. Companies conscript 'focus groups' all the time (basically a room full of random strangers who will scrutinise your product). But here's where Domino's was different. They made the feedback of their pizzas a crucial part of their marketing campaign. They showed, on nationwide television, customers consistently berating their product. (Domino's called it the 'Pizza Turnaround' campaign and you can still find it on YouTube – I'll wait here while you go take a look.) What's more, to show just how seriously they took their customers' feedback, they then took their new, reformulated pizzas back to their harshest critics' homes for a second taste test, filming the entire thing for part of the Pizza Turnaround ad campaign.

Risky strategy, but because Domino's had listened so intently to what their customers had been saying, they were confident the results would be positive. And hey presto, they were. The same men and women who had said the company was 'over' and that their pizzas were 'rubbery' were caught on camera evangelising about the product.

Within three months, Domino's share price had soared and sales of Domino's pizza in the aftermath of the campaign skyrocketed, breaking all industry records for same-store sales growth in the first quarter following the launch.

Domino's is now hailed as one of the most successful turn-arounds of any company in history. Fluke? Or was it their ability to put themselves into the discomfort zone of critical feedback that got them there? To figure that one out, we need to talk to someone who forces people to throw themselves into the feedback firing line every single day.

ENTERING THE FEEDBACK ZONE

Tasha Eurich is something of a feedback expert. Most days you will find her sitting with a frowning CEO hunched over his or her desk, perplexed as to what they are doing wrong. And, in her lovely, warm smiley way, she will tell them.

She's not always popular for this reason. After all, nobody likes to hear all the ways in which they're failing at their job, particularly not those at the top of their game. After all, if they need improvement, how did they get to be the boss in the first place?

Tasha sees this sort of confusion all the time. In her fifteen years as an organisational psychologist she has been flown around the world to work with leaders who have never been given feedback. That's a problem not only for them but also for the people and the companies they lead.

'So many of us use the excuse that we're waiting for feedback as an excuse to not seek it out,' she tells me. 'People often think if no one has told them then they're probably not doing anything wrong. For example, I once coached a man in his fifties who was by all accounts a terrible leader. One of the things he told me when I was giving him this feedback was: "How have I been doing this for twenty or thirty years and nobody has ever told me.'"

Here's why: entering the 'feedback zone' is hard and scary. 'The same reasons we don't ask for feedback are the same reasons we don't volunteer it,' Tasha tells me. 'It's evolved over time back to the days when we were hunter-gatherers, living in groups. If the group had voted us off the island, to use the more modern term, we would probably have died. As a result, we have evolved these social impulses. First of all, we don't want to learn from the group that it doesn't like us. Secondly, other people don't want to rock the boat by giving it. So we're living this charade. And it's stopping us from getting feedback that could help us be much more successful.'

A great example of where feedback has built better, stronger, more successful individuals is in sport. Take tennis players, for example: today some of the game's most celebrated players are also its oldest. Roger Federer, one of the tennis world's most artful and skilful players, is also one of its oldest (in 2017 Federer was one of the oldest players to have *ever* won Wimbledon). In fact, take a look at the age of most of the super-elite tennis players participating in today's top-tiered competitions – Andy Murray (30), Jürgen Melzer (36), Serena Williams (37) and sister Venus Williams (38). Thirty years ago, tennis players that had been on the circuit for almost a decade were considered 'veterans'. That or 'over'. Is it pure coincidence that some of the best players in the world are also the oldest to have participated at grand-slam competitive level? What is going on?

The answer is: feedback. It's notable that all the players I have mentioned came up through the ranks at a time when elite coaching was the norm. That means these players have been able to perform better and for longer because of the constant feedback they have benefitted from. In fact, the introduction of elite coaches into the world is perhaps one of the contributing factors as to why sportsmen and women now outperform those athletes that came before them (and have longer, more prosperous careers). It's not that they are any more talented but because they are forced into the discomfort feedback zone time and time again. And that results in one thing: getting better.

THE DISCOMFORT COACH

Today we might be used to the sight of a post-race athlete surrounded by a phalanx of shell-suited coaches whispering sweet nothings into their ears, but it has not always been this way.

Back in the 1970s, tennis players turned up to Wimbledon, played the game and whoever was the more talented player, and had put the most practice in, won. Simple. Games were shorter. Athletes had more injuries and careers were ended around the age of twenty-seven. But in the early 1980s something started to change. Coaches came on the scene. Many of them were not even former athletes, just men who had taught the game for years. Some of the more senior players started to work closely with them: Jimmy Connors, Martina Navratilova and John McEnroe. And something remarkable happened. They started to get better. Not marginally better, but significantly better.

Their serves were sharper. Their backhands harder. Their endurance levels higher and better than ever before.

Now the world's very best champions (who enjoy longer careers than their peers from previous decades, and can also play more extended and physically demanding games) have gone one step further and employ 'supercoaches'. These are former tennis champions turned professional coaches, who not only have an immaculate technical grasp of the game, but also a brilliant mental understanding too. Andy Murray won Wimbledon and reached the World Number one ranking when he took on former Wimbledon champion Ivan Lendl as his coach. Stefan Edberg helped Roger Federer win eleven tournaments in his thirties, while Novak Djokovic worked with Boris Becker – the youngest player ever to win Wimbledon, at age 17 – for three years, winning six Grand Slams under his tutelage.

Is it possible that one person could make such a difference to another's performance? The answer, it appears, is 'yes'. By having an impartial source give consistent feedback on everything from how a player holds their racket to even how they breath and think when they're coordinating a volley has significant effects on a player's performance.

Coaching has now become big business. There are career coaches, athletic coaches, coaches for confidence, coaches for fat loss – you name it – and they are people specifically employed for their analytical feedback. Many people have experienced enormous growth simply by having a coach give them feedback on their performance, whether that's how they perform on a gym floor (sure a personal trainer's job is to motivate, but it's also about giving constant feedback) to how they behave in the office.

I have had friends whose careers have been transformed by the addition of a career coach, for example. One friend – an exceptional leader by all accounts – whose weakness was her inability to hide her emotions when someone made her mad (which happened on the hour, every hour, her coach had to break it to her) is now as calm and measured as the Dalai Lama. And she has just landed a huge promotion just six months after employing said coach.

But I hear you: who can afford a coach? And who has the time? And, if we're being really honest here, unless you're a CEO at the top of your game, doesn't the concept of an employed coach seem just a little bit excessive, especially if, like most of the world, you're still overdrawn weeks before payday.

Here's the good news. Most of us have a coach within our midst – that person who has the rare ability to look at our behaviours and performance through unfiltered eyes. This person is able to give you the feedback you need, while also not putting you through the depths of hell in order to get it. You don't need a lot of time with them, it's completely free and, the best bit, it can improve your relationship with that person too. So how do you find this mythical person? Chances are you already know them.

THE CARING COACH

In 2012 athletes from across the globe boarded flights bound for Brazil. Their destination: the Olympic games in Rio de Janeiro. Most of them had been coached up to their eyeballs: hours and hours of advice from an impartial, by-standing coach who had spent the last year monitoring and analysing their technique and performance. They were ready. Or at least as ready as they were ever going to be.

And yet, weeks later many of those same athletes came away empty-handed, while other athletes competing in the same arena at the same discipline took home medals. Of course, in some cases the better, more naturally talented and more experienced athlete won, and people could live with that. But what about those winners who, on paper, looked identical in terms of skill, talent and training to the losers?

This is exactly what researchers at Bangor University in Wales have been investigating for some time. What, they wondered, made one set of elite athletes win medals while another set (with the same experience, same level of talent and the same amount of groundwork) didn't win any at all? What, in other words, makes a 'super-elite' athlete? The answer, many believe, was down to the *style* of coaching they received.

All the athletes, when questioned, said they received adequate technical support from their coaches, but the super-elite athletes also took great emotional support from their coaches. In other words, their coaches acted as a sort of 'surrogate' parent, motivating, encouraging and offering critical feedback.

This is where Tasha Eurich comes back in. Sure, you can get feedback from anyone and anywhere, she says, but the best feedback comes from someone she describes as a 'loving critic': 'When we ask for feedback it's almost always never as bad as we fear it might be. It's not going to be an indictment of us as a person (especially) if we're getting it in the right way and we're asking the right person.'

In her exceptional book, *Insight*, Tasha studied dozens of exceptional leaders. Those she found to be the most effective leaders were, unsurprisingly, those who asked for constant feedback. But what intrigued her most of all was who *exactly* they were asking for it from.

'One of the things that surprised me when I did my research [about these leaders] was just how picky they were about the people they sought feedback from. I expected the opposite. For most of them it's less than a handful of people. You have to be really sure that these people have our best interests at heart. After all, not all feedback is intended to help.'

You'll know this from 'unhelpful' feedback you've had from colleagues with an agenda. Them, or people with zero clue. (If you've ever had feedback from a distant relative or friend who suddenly feels the need to wade in to how you deal with your work colleagues without having any idea about the world in which you work and operate, then you'll know what I'm talking about.)

Eurich says that to get impartial, qualified feedback you need someone who not only has your best interests at heart (and no, not your mother), but someone who is also strong enough and emotionally removed enough from you to offer proper *critical* feedback. While she calls these people 'loving critics', I call them your 'care coaches'.

I have one of these at work. She is in the same offices as me and therefore has a knowledge of the industry in which I move, but I don't work with her on a day-to-day basis. She is someone I consider a friend, yes, but not an exceptionally close one. She is tough and, some in the company would say, 'brutally' honest, but I also know from past behaviour that she has my best interests at heart. That's why, when she gives me feedback, I know it is done with zero agenda. I also know her advice will entail only a very brief moment of discomfort. When she sits me down, I make sure I have a cup of tea to hand and a notepad; they help me get through those few seconds when she runs through things like: 'You know you can come across as a bit harsh sometimes, right?'

As Eurich says: 'Loving critics are the best. If you get feedback from them then you should investigate it. If you get feedback from someone who isn't a loving critic, then you should check it with your loving critic.'

HOW TO FIND YOUR CARE COACH

Hopefully by now you've realised the importance of feedback. Your next step? To seek out the person/persons who are going to give it to you.

Rule number one: no matter how brilliant your sister/mother/partner is, they are not this person. They are too bound up with your emotional life to be completely impartial. (Or a simpler rule of thumb: if this person has ever seen you in a state of undress/on the toilet at any point in your life, then they are not the right person for the job.) Instead, think about those friends or colleagues who have known you for at least a couple of years. You want someone who understands the sort of person you are (ideally, both at work and outside it, which could mean two 'care coaches' and that's okay). That's because their feedback has to at least be realistic. For example, telling an introvert that they need to speak up more and be louder in social situations is no use to anyone.

Also, think about someone who you want to know better; coaching can become a very intimate experience (no, not in that way) and will invariably bring you closer together. A friend or colleague you have known for a number of years is always a good bet. Tasha's 'loving critic' is an old friend called Mike – someone who not only cares about her but who, rather more crucially, can also stand up to her: 'He once told me, "Tasha, I love you in person, but I hate you online." It was really actionable advice. I realised I didn't have to use my personal Facebook page to list all my work accomplishments. Wow – what a concept!'

If you want to work on your performance at work then a work colleague is going to be a good option. But a word of advice: don't choose someone who reports directly to you. My gut feeling is that it blurs the lines of hierarchy. It's very difficult to manage someone who just days earlier saw you teary-eyed over your inability to lead effectively. Common sense, really, but *just saying*. Neither should you go for someone who *used* to work with you. People change from job to job and behave differently when put under a new set of conditions and responsibilities. Though there will be some similarities, I am almost certainly a different leader as an editor than as a features director, when the pressure points and demands were different.

My advice: someone who works beside you but in a different department is a wise start. You want them to have some awareness of what you're like on the job but not too much. And like I said, definitely not someone who has ever seen you undressed.

HOW LONG AND HOW OFTEN?

Let's just address the elephant in the room for a minute: no one *wants* to do this. It's hard. Getting feedback, even from someone you really, *really* like, is akin to having hot wax dripped on a sunburned arm. You have to push through that. I say this because for the first few sessions you will try and push back the regularity of these feedback sessions. I know I tried to do this with my coach. It's human nature. The human brain defends itself from two things: exposure and criticism. You're getting two lots of bang for your buck and that's hard – at first.

My advice is for both of you to agree a time at the beginning – say, thirty minutes every few weeks. These sessions do not need to be long and, in fact, as time goes by, my advice would be to make them as short as possible. But you can only do this once you're comfortable with the discomfort of feedback. The key is to remember that the discomfort will be brief – only a few seconds in most cases as your 'care coach' raises an aspect of your personality or performance at work that you were, until that moment, blissfully unaware of. But the more you get comfortable with it, the easier it will become. So much so, that pretty soon absorbing feedback from your care coach will be as effortless as breathing.

It's also worth remembering that you don't have to commit to this for the rest of your life, but if you're going through a tough patch you may want to keep your 'care coach' relationship going, at least until you feel like you've sailed out of your tough patch. After that, most 'care coaches' stay in your life.

You can call on them when you need to and hopefully, in time, you can repay the favour.

The next question: where to do it. That's up to you really, but nothing too formal. You need to be in a relaxed enough environment to take in what they're saying. I also think a public space is good because it forces you to listen. If you disagree you can't suddenly stand up and walk out or, worse, argue about it. Tasha advises having a 'dinner of truth' – basically a low-key meal together where you're relaxed enough to digest what the other person is telling you.

I do mine over breakfast in a small café where the coffee is strong and the lighting is flattering. You want to be in the best possible mindset, after all, if you're going to endure a personal take-down. Mornings tend to work best for me too, because you're invariably not worn down by the day yet. I am convinced that you need to be in a strong place mentally before you can fully absorb feedback. (Taking it in after a long day in the office when you've already been screamed at by your boss several times? Not a good idea.)

HOW DO YOU WANT IT?

Be specific

If you're vague and expansive about what you're asking, for instance: 'Can I have some feedback on my leadership style', then you'll get a vague and expansive answer in return. Go into this with a clear idea of exactly what you want to know, such as: 'I feel I might be a bit heavy-handed with how I give criticism. What do you think?' That will make your care coach focus in much more acutely on the topic in hand. (If you're very organised you can always tell your care coach what you want to talk about a few days beforehand, so that they have time to think it through.)

Be succinct

There's only so much bad news the human spirit can take. So go easy on yourself. Don't expect your care coach to give you a complete rundown of all the things you're failing at. You'll feel despondent, they'll feel an arsehole and chances are you won't meet again. Instead, ask them to give three examples (positive and negative) of how you're doing. This is just the right amount to ask them to elaborate on. It's also just the right amount for you to process. This might be how you give criticism at work, or the way you speak in front of a crowd. The point is, don't be too ambitious in each session.

Be strong

You're not there to defend yourself. You're there to listen. Smile when they give you feedback. Nod. Show you're attending to what they're telling you and that you appreciate it, even if your soul is melting inside. It's hard for them too and you want them to be as open as possible with you. They will only keep doing this if they feel comfortable. In other words, the more comfortable they feel, the more discomfort you will feel. But only at first. This will get easier. Trust me.

Take it all in

Recording this is often a good idea. I know, I know … it sounds creepy, but often we forget the smallest details when we're listening and writing things down. Play back the conversation a couple of times afterwards so that you absorb all the information.

Say thank you

Oh yes, and no matter how much you hate what they're telling you, remember that it's probably as hard for them to say it as it is for you to listen. Be grateful. Smile. Send them a bunch of flowers with a considered note once you've processed everything – the next day is usually a good idea. Because the greatest feedback they can get from you is that you're listening.

7

FINDING INSPIRATION IN CONSTRAINT

Why discomfort gives you the creative edge

The general assumption is that some people are born with a creative mindset, while others aren't. Growing up, my elder sister was always seen as 'the creative one' in the family. She wrote dazzling stories that seemed to come from a highly developed imagination, while I, on the other hand, was seen as more methodical. Ideas came slowly to me and invariably with some degree of difficulty. As such, I was seen as having more of an 'analytical' mindset. It is why, for many years, I thought I would be suited to life as a lawyer or perhaps an accountant. Journalism, a trade that relies on hugely creative thinking, wasn't even on my radar until many years later.

And yet today I edit a national magazine. My stock in trade is ideas, and consequently my days are spent coming up with new and original concepts that people have never heard of before (or at least that's what we try to do!). On paper, you would say I am a 'creative', but the truth is I'm not – not in the traditional sense anyway. I still can't pluck ideas out of mid-air or think of high-concept notions with a moment's notice. (Annoyingly, my sister still can and has about seven different *new* business ideas every time I see her.)

But arguably I *am* creative. It's just that I come to my creativity through a different doorway. It's the same creative doorway through which many people arrive at their best original work, and certainly the route by which many of the world's most famous creatives arrive at their best ideas. And that door is the one that opens into our discomfort zone. It is here, when the pressure is dialled up and constraint looms large, that we are forced to dig deep for inspiration. The composer Igor Stravinsky once said: 'The more constraints one imposes, the more one frees one's self . . . ', and this is true for everyone, from film directors and great artists to musicians and, yes, even magazine editors.

Remember how I told you that *Women's Health* was started with few resources and just two members of staff? That was no understatement. On day one I arrived at the office – a back room just off Oxford Street – with an eight-week deadline in which to create an entirely new magazine using a team who were as inexperienced as I was. With minimal money, time and people we were forced to be more creative with our ideas.

I will never forget the time we needed an image to accompany a story on breast health. Most pictures of this nature are high-end fashion images, which are invariably prohibitively expensive. So what did we do? We took an aerial picture of our intern's bare knees with the toe caps of a pair of nude shoes poking out from beneath them. Imagine if you will what that looks like. Got it? We took that image and blew it up as big as we could across the page so that it looked like a giant pair of bare breasts. It was audacious, it was funny and it set the creative tone for how we worked with visuals for the rest of our days there.

One of the things discomfort does is force you to make a decision. When things are comfortable you weigh up *all* the opportunities and that can often be deadly. By being over-whelmed by choice you can often end up going with the most conventional option. Convention is safe, sure, and convention is certainly comfortable. But convention rarely elicits true cre-ativity. That's because true creativity requires originality, and originality often comes from a place of discomfort.

Frank Gehry has built everything from the Guggenheim Museums in Bilbao and Abu Dhabi to Euro Disney and Facebook's West Campus. The Canadian architect is seen as one of the world's most creative pioneers, his buildings true flights of fantastical imagination that have each become huge tourist attractions. But Gehry's designs do not come from nowhere. He has famously said that the most difficult project he ever worked on was the one where a client gave him zero constraints to work around.

'I had a horrible time with it,' he said. 'I had to look in the mirror a lot. "Who am I? Why am I doing this? What is this all about?" It's better to have some problem to work on,' he explained. 'I think we turn those constraints into action.'

Nowhere can this be seen more clearly than at the Walt Disney Concert Hall in downtown LA. It is one of the most remarkable feats of architecture ever seen and sits on 111 South Grand Avenue like a giant sliver of foil-covered chewing gum, curved in on itself many times over. It has won countless awards and has inspired dozens of buildings across the world, including Gehry's own Guggenheim Museum in Bilbao. And yet it was riddled with constraints.

For a start, the budget was not big enough. Lillian Disney, the widow of the late Walt Disney, had given $50 million towards the building, which was created as an homage to Walt Disney's love of the creative arts. But the underground garage alone cost $110 million. Gehry had to relook at the original plans, ditching the stone exterior he had originally planned for the now iconic silver industrial-steel façade.

He had another problem: the acoustics. This was, after all, a music hall. Gehry therefore had to build the hall as a series of layers – revolutionary in its design and execution at the time. And there was one more challenge to add to the mix: the city's grid system. Gehry, unlike many architects, often designs with children's wooden building blocks. However, Gehry's blocks wouldn't work with the grid system in that part of downtown LA. Given he couldn't change the grid system, he had to work around it. The result: he created a flower-like structure that is all shapes and curves and angles and is quite unlike any other building in America. Gehry's most famous building, then, was created around constraints. If not for these the Walt Disney Concert Hall would have looked very different – and, I hazard a guess, not nearly as wonderful.

I'm sure you've been paralysed by too much freedom. I see it all the time with my team. Give a writer a loose story idea and see them struggle for days. Hand them a tight brief with a very strict angle and watch them hunch over their desk and write for days on end. It's the same with most things. We can become overburdened by choice – paralysed by it in fact. We talk about 'creative freedom' all the time, the idea that the best ideas come when you can do absolutely anything you want. 'Blue sky thinking' you might have heard it called by some berk in a pinstripe suit. Dream big! Don't be limited! Think outside the box! These are the dictums we have been fed for years. And yet, often too much freedom can be the very thing that limits us.

When I was younger I would never get my coursework in in good time. I was always the person who left it until the very last minute, pulling an all-nighter, scribbling away until the very end. I didn't love working like this, by the way. Not one bit. But I found it got the best results. Seriously. I tried on many occasions to be organised, to get my essays in weeks before the deadlines. But every time I did I found the same thing: I just didn't do as well.

I thought about it for years, and only recently read back many of those essays, which I still keep in a brown cardboard box up in the attic. Those that were written with plenty of time were incredibly bland. There was little original thought and certainly few big ideas within their pages. I yawned through most of them – and cringed. But those that I remember scrawling in the early hours of the morning were far more ambitious, their scope deeper and wider, their content original and brave.

And that's when it struck me. Having a limit (in this case, sheer lack of time) is what allowed me to be limitless with my thinking. This constraint did three things. First: it liberated me from thinking like everyone else, or *second-guessing* what everyone else would be writing. Two: it meant I put down bolder, more audacious ideas (had I had more time I would almost certainly have worried about whether they were too bold, most likely scrapping them for a 'safer' line of thought). Three: it made me more authentic. The strict time limit meant that I was forced to go with my gut instinct and, consequently, the idea that spoke loudest to me. And as we saw in Chapter Five, channelling your gut instinct is crucial to a successful outcome. Limits, ironically, could well be the very things that offer us limitless creativity.

I'll give you another example: Martin Luther King's 'I have a dream' speech, delivered to over 250,000 people during the 'March on Washington for Jobs and Freedom' on 28 August 1963, is one of the world's most iconic speeches. But few people know that the 'I have a dream' phrase was not actually in the original speech. As Adam Grant explains in his book *The Originals*, King had been reworking and reworking the speech over and over again, right up until the very last minute. When he walked on stage in front of the crowds that day, it was most definitely not part of the plan. Had he written his speech in advance, learned it word for word and then put it aside, who knows what would have happened that day. The likelihood is he would have stuck to the script. Instead, he delivered something far more authentic and powerful that day. Why he hadn't put this line in his originally planned speech we will never know – maybe he thought it too dramatic or too poetic. And this is one of my issues with long expanses of time and freedom. It allows you to second-guess yourself.

Steven Spielberg had a moment of limitation with his second major motion picture: *Jaws*. During filming, the mechanical shark that Spielberg had been using malfunctioned. It would be weeks before it could be fixed and up and running again for filming. The then twenty-five-year-old Spielberg didn't have the time or budget to wait, so instead he got creative. What about, he reasoned, if he didn't show the shark, but instead showed the damage it was capable of doing? So that's what he did. In what is now one of the most famous scenes, not only in the film but in cinematic history, two fishermen wait on a wooden pier. They throw out a giant piece of bait attached to a floating rubber tyre that is secured to the pier. As they wait, Spielberg cuts to the protagonist, Chief Brody, who sits in his office, idly flipping through a black-and-white book showing images of a giant great white shark. The images are grotesque and menacing. Spielberg then cuts back to the fishermen who notice that their bait has been taken and that the rubber tyre is moving rapidly through the water, pulling with it the entire pier. One man falls into the water. The next thing we see is the floating piece of pier moving swiftly towards him, accompanied by John Williams's masterful two-note musical score. 'Swim Charlie! Swim!' shouts one fisherman as Williams ratchets up the music and the fish/piece of wood moves towards the man in the water. It is masterful and terrifying at the same time. Never has a piece of driftwood looked so frightening.

Had Spielberg not been challenged by the constraints he found himself in, it's doubtful the scene would have had as much tension. As it was, he managed to create drama and suspense out of a rubber tyre, a piece of wood and an E-F-E-F bassline. It also helped Spielberg to create his signature 'tension' device. Even if you haven't seen *Jurassic Park* you will be familiar with the scene in which a trembling glass of water, accompanied by a heavy bassline, shows there is a dinosaur approaching.

Artists, too, have long known about the importance of constraints. Take the Impressionists, who created some of the most breathtaking work of the last four hundred years and yet confined themselves to the use of short brushstrokes and vivid colours. Or film director Lars von Trier, who created the school of film-directing known as Dogme 95. Dogme film-makers are forced to shoot with only hand-held cameras and without props, optical filters or special lighting – and about half a dozen other restrictions that make you wonder why anyone would take part. And yet the Dogme movement has produced some of the most inventive and critically acclaimed films of the last thirty years. (If you have never seen *Festen* or *The Idiots*, then book off a Saturday afternoon to do so now. Disclaimer: you may need a stiff drink to accompany both.)

It's not just in the world of art either. Nordstrom, the giant Canadian retail chain, has a small tech start-up within its business called the Nordstrom Innovation Lab, where each idea is given just one week to come to fruition. Apple famously had only eight months from start to shop to create the iPod (any longer and they would have missed the Christmas deadline).

But is it true? Can the discomfort of constraint really make us more creative? Can it really lead to our greatest break-throughs and our most brilliant ideas? The man who has changed the way the world dates thinks it does.

HAVING THE CONSTRAINT 'EDGE'

Tinder now connects over 24 million people a day across 196 countries on the planet. It also made Sean Rad one of the world's most successful and influential entrepreneurs. At the time of going to press, it is the second most profitable app in the world, second only to Netflix. It has birthed countless Tinder babies, thousands of Tinder marriages, hundreds of thousands of Tinder relationships and, I'd hazard a guess, a hell of a lot of sex. And yet it was born from discomfort after discomfort after discomfort.

Not that you'd know to look at Rad. He's in his early thirties, yet has the calm disposition of a fifty-year-old chess player, his occasional flyaway hands the only giveaway of his shimmering youth.

And yet it wasn't always this way. What many don't know is that Tinder was created from a brief moment of discomfort: twenty-three crazed days over the long hot summer of 2012, in fact. It was a ragtag team of five twenty-somethings who worked round the clock in an airless office with just a couple of couches and a single coffee table for company. They had little experience, few contacts and not nearly enough time on their side.

Every day there were dozens of changes to the app, mistake after mistake and blind alley after blind alley. There was feedback from the data, feedback from the rapidly expanding group of users and feedback from one another. Soon, three hours' sleep a night was standard as servers crashed, better, stronger ideas blossomed and the noise of other people's suggestions engulfed them like a forest fire. It was one giant discomfort zone ... and it forced them to think and behave in ways they could never have imagined.

With no marketing plan or budget, they deployed a group of young, street-smart interns to hit the streets and talk about this cool new dating app no one had heard of. On the rare occasions Rad and the team would leave the office to brainstorm over beers, they would sit on roadside tables and shout out to groups of men and women: 'Hey, have you guys heard of this new dating app called Tinder?' With the couple of hundred dollars they had put aside for marketing they had a thousand fist-sized company stickers made up with Tinder's distinctive red flame. They stuck them on lampposts and bins across LA before hitting Coachella, the starry music festival in Nevada, where they fly-posted every toilet door, every sanitary bin and every unmolested surface. Soon word got out that this strange new dating app had sponsored the entire event.

Momentum started to build. And build. Within a couple of weeks they had around four hundred new users. By the end of the year they had thousands. And by the end of 2013 it was the most popular dating app in the world for anyone under thirty.

'When I look back, I think the bad moments were as much a part of the plan that got me here as the good ones – maybe even more so,' Rad tells me in his soft LA lilt. 'I also think when I look back at Tinder that the greatest ideas came from our disagreements and then talking it through. Feedback is scary and it can be disorientating, but if you are an organisation that is afraid to listen then you are never going to grow. You can't grow without mistakes. I think if you're not making mistakes then you're probably not doing anything worthwhile. Because once you make a mistake it's a piece of information you have that no one else has.' In other words, it was the most uncomfortable moments that led to the app's greatest successes.

But why is it that the discomfort of constraint leads to the most brilliant and original breakthroughs? Is it, perhaps, because our brains are hard-wired to work more effectively under these conditions? The answer, science says, is yes.

In a recent and landmark study by the University of Amsterdam, researchers set out to find how constraints cognitively affected us. They did several tests on students, which largely involved them listening to a series of words and numbers while undertaking a series of challenging anagrams. The results were myriad and remarkable. Firstly, the study found that constraints shifted the students' thought processes from localised to globalised thinking (it allowed them to make a big-picture assessment of a situation rather than a myopic one) or, as the study called it, it increased their 'perceptual scope'. And perceptual scope is crucial for ambitious, creative thinking.

So, too, is something called 'conceptual scope', which the study also found was increased when the students were faced with challenges. Conceptual scope is also integral to creative thinking, because it allows you to see a greater number of ideas and possibilities, and is therefore useful in avoiding common lines of thought. Finally the study made perhaps its most surprising finding of all: that constraints, contrary to popular belief, make us more engaged with a difficult project and therefore more likely to stick with it.

The students were all given a computer maze to complete, with some participants experiencing a blocking obstacle midway through, making it harder to escape. Afterwards they were all given a test called a 'remote associates' test, which is largely considered to be a standard measure of creativity. The students who had experienced the obstacle completed 40 per cent more of the test. In other words, the discomfort of confronting the constraint had increased their creative mindset.

8

EMBRACING SMART FAILURE

Why brilliant leaders love
the challenge of failing

On 16 December 1996 I sat bolt upright in bed, a letter between my hands. I knew what it was. After all, I had been waiting for it for years. It was a letter from Oxford University.

As far back as I can remember I have always known I would go to Oxford. That's because I have always wanted to impress my father. He was a first-wave immigrant from Pakistan and I was his third child – a shy kid who showed little academic vigour. As those of you who also come from Asian families will know, intellectual curiosity and academic results are applauded in Asian culture. It's an ongoing joke that distant uncles and aunts may not know your middle name but they will know how many GCSEs you got, what grades they were and how far ahead of the rest of the class you currently are. (All wildly over-exaggerated by your parents, of course.)

The way to impress my father, I figured, was to become

an A-grade student. And even better than that, the way to really, *really* impress him would be to be accepted into Oxford University. So that's what I focused on. From the age of thirteen I studied. And studied. And studied some more. My grades started to shift. I went from B's to A minus's. A minus's to straight A's. And finally, on GCSE day, from grade A's to a clean sweep of A-stars. My path was set. I had Oxford in my sights.

I travelled up there one cold autumnal morning, all packed and prepped for the intensive three days of interviews. I remember arriving at Worcester College, a grand, aristocratic beauty of a building, with my heart fluttering away like a hummingbird's wings. I took dinner in the large dining room, a cavernous place of ancient wood and intense formality, and recall being slightly embarrassed by my Northern twang. The interviews were conducted in front of a panel of old, grey men with devastating manners and even more devastating questions. I remember taking the train back to Salford, stepping onto the platform at Manchester Piccadilly and telling my mum it was now just a waiting game. I had a row of predicted grade A's. I had, I believed, performed immaculately. The questions the dons had thrown at me had been challenging, sure, but I had high-jumped the easier ones and majestically swerved the harder bits. It was only a matter of time.

But when I opened the letter that morning it did not contain the answer I had been expecting – the one I had anticipated for the last five years of my life. The tears fell before I even managed to read to the bottom. It was over. I had been rejected. It was early morning and still dark outside and I asked my mother not to open the curtains that day. I stayed in bed, very still beneath the sheets, for many hours after that. We didn't talk much about it. No amount of platitudes or reassuring consolations from my parents could add balm to the wound. 'There will be other universities, other opportunities ...' my father said. But to me, it was a sign: I was a failure.

I bombed out later that year. I started going out and dating older boys. I quit the punishing work schedule I had set myself for the last few years. When A-level results day came around I didn't get my predicted grades. I went out. Got drunk. Decided I would just go to any university that would have me. It took many years for the sting of failure to subside.

That brief moment of discomfort, that one line in the letter which read, 'We're sorry to inform you that ...' changed the course of my life. At the time I thought it had changed the course of my life for the worst. Now, looking back twenty years later, I see that the deeply uncomfortable failure that I had been forced to come to terms with that day was actually one of the defining moments of my life.

Most of us have been brought up to believe that failure is best if it's somebody else's problem. Failing at exams. Failing at fitting in at school. Failing at work. Nowhere in the history of peoplekind was failure ever heralded as an aspiration. This cultural mindset has led to generations of men and women with something called 'failure anxiety' – an aversion to ever trying anything new or too challenging for fear of fucking it all up. But there's a big problem with that: by fearing the discomfort of failure we miss the opportunities needed to move our lives forward. After all, you can never make the big, bold leaps required of true success if you're too scared of the possible fall.

The dial, however, is starting to shift. In campuses across America, for example, some academics are starting to notice a problem with their high-achieving students. At universities like Stanford, Harvard and Princeton (the Oxfords and Cambridges of America), most students are faultless on paper – the sort of kids who have spent a lifetime leading the soccer team, out-debating the *entire* debate team and tinkling their way to Grade Five in piano in their spare time. Their lives are made up of an ever-escalating succession of conventional success metrics. And that's a problem, because these same kids are the very ones who are rocked by the smallest struggles: not getting into a university club, not getting on to the course they wanted. These everyday tribulations, tutors were finding, were leading to depression, anxiety and even tearful sessions in the university counselling rooms. It was such an issue that Stanford and Harvard universities came up with a term to describe it: 'failure deprived'. Here were young men and women who, the more outstanding they appeared on paper, the more difficult they found it to deal with life's teeniest obstacles.

In response, Stanford started an initiative called the Resilience Project, where prominent alumni from the university admitted to hardships along the way. 'It was an attempt to normalise struggle,' Ms Lythcott-Haims, the former dean of freshmen at the university told the *New York Times*. Others soon followed. Harvard now has a flourishing initiative called the Success-Failure Project – an amalgamated collection of failure stories from across the campus. Princeton has its own variation too: the Perspective Project, an on-campus space where students come together to talk about failures and things they're generally having difficulty with, which they are then encouraged to share through writing, videos and 'creative expression'. Smith College for Women in Massachusetts has gone one step further with a programme called Failing Well. Students who choose to join the programme are handed a certificate on their first day which reads: 'You are hereby authorized to screw up, bomb or fail at one or more relationships, hook-ups, friendships, texts, exams, extracurriculars or any other choices associated with college . . . and still be a totally worthy, utterly excellent human.'

Things are changing in the wider ether too. Google, once famous for only taking the very shiniest students from nearby Stanford University, is now casting its net further afield. Deloitte & Touche, one of America's largest recruitment consultants, used to concentrate their efforts on fresh-faced, failure-free MBA graduates. Now they look to those in their thirties and beyond, those with a bit more of a 'compromised' employment history. (Jim Wall, the one-time hiring manager for Deloitte, said: 'We need people with practice and experience and, hey, if you are out there competing in the world, life happens.')

Even at *Cosmopolitan* we accept that perfection doesn't always make the candidate best for the job. For many years, applications for our prestigious features intern position (a year-long paid internship programme on the magazine where the chosen candidate is essentially schooled in how to become a writer and editor) required a journalism diploma. Now we just want fearless writers. And fearlessness, in my experience, often comes from being beaten around a little bit. It comes from having tasted struggle and failure. It comes from having been grazed by life's sharp edges, rather than shackled by success. It comes from having tasted the discomfort of failure.

The richest man in the world has failed more times than he can remember. Jeff Bezos, the black-eyed, shiny-pated multi-billionaire behind Amazon is pretty open about it too. He reckons he's had billions of dollars' worth of failure at Amazon, with dozens of unsuccessful launches and projects over the last two decades. These include, though are not limited to, Amazon Auctions (his answer to eBay, which lasted all of two years before they cut off the oxygen supply), as well as Amazon Destinations, their stab at an online travel website – again, shuttered after only six months in operation. And anyone remember Amazon's first smartphone, the Fire Phone? A total, colossal wipeout that cost the company hundreds of millions of dollars.

You'd think most people would look back through that catalogue of disasters and think: 'Hmm . . . this digital thing? Maybe it's not working out too well for me. Perhaps it's time to try something different.' But not Bezos. He wants more failures and he wants them faster and bigger than ever before.

'If you think [the Fire Phone] is a big failure, we're working on much bigger failures right now. And I am not kidding. And some of them are going to make the Fire Phone look like a tiny little blip,' he told the *Washington Post* shortly after the phone was discontinued.

Bezos has a love affair with failure. Of the last twenty annual shareholder letters he has written, almost every one has made some reference to failure. What's more, in the last few years Bezos has had a tendency to hire people who have failed rather than succeeded to fill some of his most senior management roles. A case in point: Amazon Fresh, which is run by the top executives from Webvan, the car crash of a food delivery company that raised $800 million in capital back in 2001 and lost it all.

But why? How can failing, not once but again and again *and* again be a recipe for success? Is Bezos actually one of life's biggest losers who, despite his track record of failures, has somehow managed to throw enough ideas out there to have a couple stick? Or is there genius method in his apparent madness? Is the great unspoken secret to the world's richest man's wealth and success actually . . . *failure*?

EMBRACING 'SMART FAILURE'

Of course, not all failure is created equal. The type of failure Jeff Bezos obsesses over is not the type of failure that Joe Bloggs from Year Five exhibited when he flunked every class by not doing any revision. Failure by carelessness, lack of effort or lack of skill is bad failure. But failure that comes about because of trying something new? That's part of the process. Failure that happens on the frontier of innovation? That's to be expected. Failure that is a consequence of taking a bold risk that no one has ever dared to take before? That's to be applauded.

People like Jeff Bezos have to be comfortable with failure because they are constantly pushing the limits of possibility. (At the time of writing Amazon are looking into a delivery service where your Amazon items are left *inside* your actual home. Hands up who thinks there's going to be some failures on *that* front?) And when you do that, when you attempt to go where no one else has gone before, you have no template of what to do and no code of best practices learned along the way. That means you are going to stumble. Probably quite a lot. 'Failure comes part and parcel with invention. It's not optional. We understand that and believe in failing early and iterating until we get it right,' Bezos wrote in one of his shareholder letters.

The idea of failing early is a smart one. If you fail early, the size of the failure is reduced. It also lands a lot quieter, softening the blow to both your reputation and confidence. Many of the world's most famous brands know this. Why else do you think beauty and fashion companies have so many 'limited edition' products? They are a test to see how the market responds. If they do well, they launch properly (Tom Ford's Soleil Blanc perfume, Lush's Scrubbee Scrub Bomb and Charlotte Tilbury's Pillow Talk all started life as limited-edition products). And if they don't? (Anyone remember Dove's Limited Edition Real Beauty Bottles – packaging launched in 2006 and designed to look like 'real' women's bodies, except there were only seven sizes, which consequently made everyone feel bad about themselves?) The failures are chalked down to 'experience'.

Pop-ups work in the same way. The concept is simple: test small and test early. Some of London's most popular restaurants began life as rough and ready pop-ups, making as many mistakes as they did innovations on their 'semi-permanent' shop floors. MEATliquor, now a restaurant chain with eight locations, a turnover of £15 million and a queue round the block every weeknight started life as a £3000 second-hand burger van parked up in a South London car park every weekend. Pizza Pilgrims, one of the UK's fastest-growing independent pizza chains and said to be one of the best places in the world to eat pizza, started even smaller.

The two brothers behind the brand, Thom and James Elliot, quit their media jobs to start making Neopolitan-style pizzas out of the back of a three-wheel Piaggio Ape van parked in London's Berwick Street market in 2012. James told me they made '*so* many mistakes' early on. These included, though again are not limited to, a sign designed by Thom's girlfriend that featured a rolling pin (turns out no one uses a rolling pin to make pizza in Naples); losing a substantial amount of their scant funds by buying cheap refrigeration units ('Never trust a guy you just met in Soho who says "I've got some fridges going cheap!"'), as well as a complex paying system involving tins and marbles, which they thought would be revolutionary but just 'confused everyone'. But, James admits, it was the mistakes made early on and made small that meant they were able to move so quickly (and successfully) later on.

Canadian leisurewear brand Lululemon has even made a live retail experience out of the company's dedication to constant experimentation. Lululemon Lab is called a 'design concept store' and is essentially a shop in which customers can see and interact with the designers as they sample new, limited-edition pieces. If something's a runaway success, the design and materials used start to filter through into the main stores. If they're not, they're left as a limited piece in the consumer's wardrobe. In other words, it's failure redressed as exciting innovation, where everyone benefits.

LEARNING FROM FAILURE

But simply making a bunch of mistakes as you experiment doesn't guarantee success. Failure only truly works to our advantage when we dare to examine what went wrong in the first place. And that means stepping into your discomfort zone. Not sure how you respond to failure? Then see if you identify with any of the characteristics below.

The failure averse

You're the sort of person who doesn't experience failure. At least not consciously. That's because you never put yourself in a position to fail. You have a comfortable life. And you have a comfortable life because you consistently swerve the discomfort of failure. You do this by keeping your life goals very vague – that way you don't have any criteria by which to judge whether you have failed or not. But in doing that you never really move anywhere, which is in itself failing, but failing every single day. Sounds complicated. It's not: your fear is failure itself.

The failure hesitant

You're not afraid of making mistakes because you understand that they are often a necessary consequence of experimentation. In this way you're *generally* okay with discomfort. You are a bit like me at the poolside: you're prepared to go through with the discomfort of getting to the pool's edge, but you stop short of going through with the full immersion. And that's a serious loss.

What happens is this: you're not afraid of making mistakes, but you are too scared to wade right into the discomfort of discovering the reasons for those mistakes in the first place, afraid of what failure might reveal about you. You chalk up problems to a failure to follow procedures rather than any mistake on your part. And so you end up making the same ones over and over again.

By truffling down through a problem, trying to get to the nub of what went wrong, you may stumble upon your own inadequacies. And that's hard. That's the part of the discomfort zone you're unwilling to travel into. And yet it's the bit you probably need to move around in the most.

The failure brave

You embrace failure. You recognise that mistakes are often the inevitable fallout from innovation. However, you also recognise that the only way to reduce the number of mistakes made going forward is to comb through the ones you have already made – ideally, as quickly as possible. As a consequence of this, you are hyperaware of where your own fault lines lie. To safeguard against these, and to ensure you never repeat the same mistake twice (which you rarely do), you surround yourself with those who have strengths where you have blind spots.

Recognise yourself in any of those? Or maybe you are shades of all three? Whichever, the bottom line is this: in order to reap the rewards of failure (of which there are many) you need to know how to fail *properly*.

MAKING PERFECT MISTAKES

Sim Sitkin is a professor of management at Duke University. As such, he's spent a lot of his career looking at how people at the top of their professions fail. And he has worked out this: the most successful people make 'intelligent failures'. Why, you may be wondering, do they need to make mistakes at all if they're at the top of their game? Well, Sitkin was looking at those whose projects or professions depended on new information or radical innovation that had never been done before. That might be someone who is starting a new business in an unknown sector, someone who is testing a brand-new product or simply someone who wants feedback from customers where there never has been any before. The point is they have no research or experience on which they can fall back on, because there's no template. Because of that, there's a high chance they might get some things wrong. And if they know they're going to make mistakes, how, then, do they make sure they make them in the best possible way?

MAKING FAILURE ACCEPTABLE

Thankfully, the Western world is starting to talk about failure a lot more. There are companies in Silicon Valley (where else?) who hold 'failure parties' where employees are encouraged to celebrate their greatest failures. And then, of course, there's Failcon – an annual conference that celebrated failure in the tech world, held every year since 2009, and only shuttered in

2014 because the organisers felt people were sick of talking about failure. But despite the growing conversation around it, the fact remains: when the shit hits the fan, the instincts of most people is to find out A: Who did the shit? And B: Who in God's name provided the fan?

The reason we're so nervous around failure is simple: we have a deeply entrenched 'blame game' culture. Instead of looking at all the steps that led to a particular problem, we search for the culprit behind it. The problem with doing that is that it oversimplifies the problem and failures are never truly down to just one person. But also, and this is a real issue, blaming someone for the mistake shuts down conversation around it. There are two reasons for this. First, think about all the times in your life that you have been blamed for something. What was the best way to deal with it? In my experience, trying to explain how it happened is usually met with deep scowls and folded arms. It is seen as trying to 'justify' your behaviour, rather than explain the steps that led up to it (which, as we'll discover, is exactly what we should be doing!). No, the best way to usually deal with 'blame game' culture is to suck it up, apologise and then wait for the words: 'Good, now let's all move on and forget this ever happened.' Which, again, is exactly the opposite of what we should be doing.

What's more, blaming someone for failures makes people less likely to ever want to take a risk for fear of being casti-gated if it doesn't work out. You see this time and again in the reality show *The Apprentice*, when, on week one, none of the contestants volunteer to be team leader for fear of being blamed for the 'failure of the task'. I often think it bizarre that a reality show whose very purpose is to find the country's smartest entrepreneur fires the people who pursue bold leads and take daring risks in order to try and win a task. After all, those are the very tenets on which true entrepreneurship is based. By making others fearful of the consequences of failure all you ultimately do is set yourself up for bigger failure as no one will push forward, make big decisions or take the sort of risks needed for great success.

So how do you make failure acceptable? You talk about it. And you talk about it in an unemotional manner. You look at *what* went wrong rather than *who* was responsible for it going wrong. In Japan teachers often set children very difficult problems to solve in order that some of them will fail. But, whereas in Western schools the child who gets the right answer is singled out and the ones who get it wrong are shamed, in Japan it works slightly differently. Here, the child who is struggling to find the right answer is the one who is singled out. The other children in the class are then encouraged to help this child find the right answer. They must talk about it, fathom it out together and never, ever demonise the child in question for failing to get there by him/herself. By talking so openly about failure, they take the discomfort out of it.

The car company Toyota operates in a similar way. So famous, in fact, has this Japanese car company become for its approach to failure that it has a whole system, known as the Toyota Production System, which has been adopted across the world. The system is very simple: if a Toyota worker spots an issue on the production line, they pull a cord called an andon cord. If the problem cannot be solved in under a minute then the entire production line is stopped (often at huge cost to the company) until the problem can be understood and fixed. This constant assessment of even the teeniest failure means the company makes lots of small, incremental improvements.

You not only have to remove the shame from those who fail as a by-product of 'calculated' experimentation (obviously rewarding failure due to careless experimentation is not what we're focused on here), but you have to reward those who spot failure early on.

Yet, again, we have a tendency as a culture to brand those who spot mistakes as 'irritants' at best, or 'not with the group' at worst. They become a dark cloud over an office culture that genuflects at the altar of a 'Let's smash this!' attitude. But unless they are actually human fire extinguishers putting out any little flame of optimism in the office (and these people do exist) then we should not only listen to these people, but we should reward them. Some companies instigate a system called 'blameless reporting' where workers raise concerns over mistakes anonymously. While this would certainly encourage more people to spot failure early on, I tend to think that creating a culture where failure, and the spotting of 'escalating failure', is normalised is a better long-term solution.

If you run a small team, are a manager at a big company or perhaps have your own start-up, then another way to encourage open conversation about failure is to have an allotted time per week when everyone is encouraged to talk about it. Sometimes it just takes one other person to start the conversation before others will wade in. Just make sure no one is allowed to apportion blame, only to talk about the problem and a solution – ideally a solution that the team has come up with *together*.

FAILURE ANALYSIS

How do you learn from your failures? How do you wring them dry of every valuable piece of information? The truth is that most failures are complex and come about because of a number of reasons. This is why it's a good idea to gather together a SWAT team to dissect exactly what went wrong. Ideally, you'll need those who have different skill sets to yourself and one another, because sometimes it takes someone with a different perspective to recognise a fault that you may have been blind to.

It's also worth noting that you should try and recognise what went right as well. Not only will it lift everyone's spirits, but often recognising what went your way (as well as what didn't) ensures it happens again. All too often if things go right we just accept this as the norm, but that's not always the case. Everything should be dissected in order to learn. Both the good and the bad.

If you're working alone, or maybe if you're trying to figure out what went wrong in a relationship, then you may not feel comfortable having a team around you poring over your most intimate moments. I get that. Try to write down as much as possible in that case. Again, both the good and bad. Then use a colour to represent what went wrong and what went right. (A lot of companies use this technique in their reports, using green for good, yellow for caution and red for a problem.) Highlight your failures and successes. When you come to a failure try and do as Sean Rad from Tinder does and ask yourself 'Why?' Several times. Why did this happen? What could have prevented it? Could you have done anything differently?

(This isn't victim-blaming by the way. Remember how I said you can only change what you can control? You can't control someone else's behaviour. But by modifying yours it may mean you avoid the failure altogether in the future.)

As I sit here writing this I am drinking a can of Coke Zero. I mention this because Coke Zero was born out of a failure that was thoroughly dissected. Back in 2004 Coca-Cola wanted to create a drink for men aged between twenty and forty. Diet Coke was doing well, but it was more of a women's drink: the colours, the zero-calorie premise, the advertising campaign that centred around a group of hysterical women demanding a Diet Coke break after seeing a semi-naked builder. So they came up with the idea of C2. It would have half the calories and carbohydrates of regular Coke with all the taste of the real thing. And men would love it. They spent $50 million on the advertising campaign. It was stocked on shelves across the world. And it was a massive flop.

When they looked into what had gone wrong, it turned out that men did want the same traditional taste of Coke, but, just like women, they wanted no calories (and didn't really care about the carb-factor). C2 was shelved and a year later Coke Zero – now one of the brand's bestselling drinks – was launched from the mistakes learned.

The truth is this: if you want to challenge yourself, leave bold marks in the world and lead a life that is full and rewarding, then failure will play some role. Nile Rogers, one of the most successful singer-songwriters of all time, puts his phenomenal success down to the failures he has had, as well as how he has examined those failures. He, by the way, is the man behind every dance hit you can think of from the 1970s

9

DITCHING 'THE SLOG' FOR 'THE GRIND'

The difference between bad and good discomfort

When she looked out across the 5000 square feet of glossy nail counters, marble floors and smiling, lab-coated beauty therapists, she couldn't believe how far she had come. In just a few years twenty-seven-year-old Marcia Kilgore had gone from being an overworked personal trainer struggling to pay the rent on her East Village walk-up to being hailed as the toast of New York City with a business, Bliss Spa, that everyone wanted a piece of. How *exactly* did a young woman from a small suburban town in rural Canada, with no business qualifications and little experience in the beauty industry, create a $30 million cosmetic business seemingly overnight? She understood the difference between good discomfort and bad discomfort. Or, as she calls it, the difference between a 'slog' and a 'grind'.

When I say the word 'grind' what do you think of? Do you think of coffee beans being crushed under the whirling blades of a grinder? Or maybe wheat being pummelled against a stone slab? Maybe you remember your parents shaking their heads after your two-week summer holiday and saying, 'Well, I guess it's back to the "grind".' Or perhaps you think of a well-meaning teacher instructing you to 'keep your nose to the grindstone' just before exam time?

The word 'grind' suggests hard work. It suggests laborious discomfort; a relentless, repetitive series of movements or moments that result in very little. It's not a word we're fond of. If something is 'grinding work' it smacks of mind-numbing boredom. Who wants to embrace 'the grind' you're probably thinking? *You* need to embrace 'the grind'. Because it's not something to be afraid of, and it's certainly not something to dread. It is a transformative act that all great thinkers, creators and entrepreneurs go through in order to find success. Tinder's Sean Rad and his founding team of tech-musketeers? They were *all* about 'the grind'. Eric Underwood, one of the greatest dancers of our time? His entire career was based on it. As for Victoria Pendleton, the most successful British female athlete of all time? It was grind after grind after grind.

But what is 'the grind' and how can you recognise it? It's *good* discomfort. It's invigorating discomfort. It's the run-up to your breakthrough leap. The grind is you honing your skills and determining your craft without even realising it. It's less about doing the same thing over and over again, with no discernible change in direction or momentum being gathered, and is more about tiny, imperceptible reorientations being created while you work and work away, resulting in a giant, successful groundswell once you've been doing it long enough.

Sure, some people have overnight success without having committed to 'the grind', but they are rare. Rarer still are those who have immediate success and then continue on towards even greater success. Why? Because without 'the grind' there is no fallback. There is no experience to guide you on your decision-making process. There is no pattern recognition as to what works and what doesn't. The grind often feels like it's making no difference whatsoever, and in that way it can *feel* like bad discomfort, when in fact it is what makes *all* the difference.

Marcia Kilgore grew up relatively poor in Outlook, Canada, an unremarkable town in the state of Saskatchewan. Her father died when she was just eleven years old, leaving her mother, a secretary, to raise Marcia and her two siblings alone.

Marcia is in her forties now and is one of the business world's rare things: a serial entrepreneur with proven success after success. After she sold Bliss to LVMH, the luxury conglomerate that also owns Louis Vuitton, she went on to found cosmetics company Soap & Glory, which she sold several years later to British high-street retailer Boots. That could have been it for her, but instead of sitting back, dusting off her hands and counting up the profits, Marcia then did it all over again, reinvesting her money back into two new, highly 'disruptive' business ventures: FitFlop, the 'wellness' shoes that claim to give you a lower-body workout as you walk, as well as Soaper Duper, a range of environmentally friendly body products beloved by the beauty press. And in 2015 she also launched one of the most radical beauty product services ever to hit the market: Beauty Pie.

But why? Start-ups are hard, relentless work, characterised by huge amounts of discomfort. If you didn't need to throw yourself back into it, why then would you do it? The answer is that truly successful people are addicted to good discomfort. Or what Marcia calls 'the grind'.

When we meet, in a quiet health-food café in the less ritzy corner of Fulham, she is in the giddy 'start-up' phase. She had just come back from a trip to one of the Swiss factories where Beauty Pie's products are made and talks in long, melodic flows about the miraculous serums and face masks she is about to launch at bargain prices. Beauty Pie is a subscription-only beauty business model, where users pay a monthly fee and *then* get to pay factory prices for dozens of products that come from the same factories as some of your favourite designer cosmetics. Think £3.43 for a luxurious red lipstick.

Marcia explains that as a child discomfort was never far away. 'I don't think I ever felt comfortable as a child in terms of being provided for,' she explains. After her father died, although money was scarce Marcia did have smarts to fall back on. And as luck would have it, aged seventeen she gained a place at Columbia University in Manhattan. Her elder sister, who had recently moved to New York, agreed to pay the tuition fees. Marcia bought a one-way ticket to New York, landed in Manhattan and then – disaster: 'My sister had the money and then she didn't! So there I was with a one-way ticket and, well, I was basically stranded.'

She was in the very teeth of her discomfort zone. And so, as all successful people do when they find themselves in there, she had to think her way through. She had always loved exercise and so set herself up as a personal trainer. (It was the 1990s, no one was concerned with qualifications and a long list of flashy clients.) But the hours were long and the sessions exhausting. It was a *slog*.

'I'd have to get somewhere by 6.30 a.m. and I'd finish at 11 p.m. And I had to walk all the way home to the East Village because I didn't have much money and after a couple of years of doing this again and again and again I just thought, "This is not sustainable."'

That's what bad discomfort feels like: relentless. It is like the Greek myth of Sisyphus, the man who was damned for eternity to carry a boulder up a hill only for it to fall back down again. You can't see a way out unless something shifts. Marcia needed something to shift.

At the time, she had terrible acne and had gone on a crash course on how to give facials to sort out her own skin problems. But while there, she realised she could practise her new-found skills on her existing PT clients as well. ('They were very trusting. I mean, would *you*? I wouldn't!')

She rented a tiny studio in the East River Savings Bank building between Prince Street and Lafayette Street in SoHo – in the same building that Leo Castelli, one of the most famous art dealers of the time, had just taken 5000 square feet of space for his gallery.

'It was tough. My overheads on the studio were $700 a month and then, with my apartment on top of that, I needed to cover around $1500 every single month. I charged $40 for a personal training session. So that was a lot of personal training sessions before I could pay. I would then do facials all day on a Saturday and then take the laundry from the facial studio to the laundromat at night.'

To most people this would have felt relentless. It would have felt like *bad* discomfort: the back-breaking days, the constant worry about paying the rent, the endless hours of non-stop slog. But it wasn't. Why? Because she was moving forward. There was change happening. Only small moments of change, but enough for her to feel things were shifting and moving forward.

Word started to spread about this miraculous woman in SoHo who was doling out transformative facials. Kim Gordon from Sonic Youth became a client. So did Bette Midler and Demi Moore. US *Vogue* wrote a small feature about her. Oprah came. The supermodels trickled in. Soon the whole of New York was talking about Marcia Kilgore. She was just twenty-three years old. She upgraded to a bigger studio with three treatment rooms and hired a couple of members of staff to help out. The phone rang from 7 a.m. until they closed late in the evening. There was a waiting list of eighteen months – 'because if you want a facial, you want it every month and some people were saying: "Book me in every fourth Tuesday at 6.30 p.m." for two years.'

The momentum gathered so much that when Marcia found out that Leo Castelli was vacating his 5000 square foot space in the building, she decided to take over the lease. She would, she decided, open her own place. And she would call it Bliss.

Bliss Spa went on to become the most famous spa in the world, its SoHo premises booked up for months in advance.

In fact, it was such a success that, at just twenty-nine years of age, Marcia sold the business to LVMH for the then staggering amount of $30 million.

Could she have done that had she not recognised the difference between good discomfort and bad discomfort on her path to success? 'Everything should be hard, otherwise you're not doing anything. So it's always a grind if you're getting somewhere. I have slogs every day. You have them until you get into the grind. Slog improves to grind which improves to faster grind. Grind is friction. Slog is dragging.'

IDENTIFYING YOUR 'GRIND'

You see, the grind is necessary in order to make big, successful leaps. Bliss would never have been born if Marcia had not slogged away for years as a personal trainer, which in turn led to grinding away at facials, which in turn led to grinding away at creating Bliss Spa. Grind is the uphill struggle that gets you to the top of the hill. Slog is running over the same ground at the bottom of the hill and getting nowhere. Grind leads to change. Slog keeps you static.

Most successful people embrace the discomfort of 'the grind.' It is what motivates them. Some of them even find it the most enjoyable part of their job. Take Roald Dahl, the most famous children's writer of all time. He wrote over forty bestselling books and had a career that lasted from his early forties right up until he died, aged seventy-four. You would think he could dash off a couple of books a year. And the truth is, he was so well-versed in how to write books and craft characters that he probably could. But, instead, he still insisted on writing the first paragraph to each one of his books 150 times. That's right, that's not a typo: 150 times. Why would he do that when he could just relish the comfort of being able to blast off a paragraph in a few minutes? He did it because he recognised that it was the discomfort of 'grinding' away with new words, new ideas and new ways to deliver sentences that led to better books.

Radiohead, arguably one of the greatest bands of the last century, famously embrace the discomfort of 'the grind.' Like Dahl before them, they could spend a couple of hours in a studio every day, falling back on classic songwriting templates every time they have an album to put out. But they don't. To them, wasting time creating the same music they have done before would be bad discomfort, because they wouldn't see change. Instead they head to a studio – often for intense days at a time – where they 'grind' away until new sounds and forms of music come together.

They don't just sit there writing music, resting on the same patterns and beats per minute that most songs and songwriters lean towards. No, they fiddle and play and fiddle and play and, little by little, their music takes shape. It starts to change. Listen to most artists' albums and they sound kind of the same. A Justin Bieber album kind of always sounds like a Justin Bieber album. So too does a Led Zeppelin album. Their songs are always a similar length with a similar placement of choruses and chords.

But Radiohead are famous for never having produced two albums that sound alike. They choose to innovate, rather than imitate what they have done before, even if their previous album was a huge success. Case in point: their third album *OK Computer*. It was one of the most successful releases of the 1990s, but Radiohead's follow-up three years later, *Kid A*, appeared to have abandoned everything that had made them a hit on their previous album. Gone were the guitar pyrotechnics and classic songwriting structures (verse-chorus-verse) and in their place was a completely new sound suffused with electronic beats, synths and even hip hop.

I remember when it came out and the complete discombobulation of everyone I knew who had been a Radiohead fan up until that point. It took time and patience to get familiar with this new sound – its discordant beats per minute, the unusual length of each song and even the placement of the choruses and verses. But with each listen the album became more profound, more memorable and the songs better and more complex as we all adapted to this challenging new sound. Today it is universally recognised as one of the greatest albums of all time.

CAN YOU EVER LEARN TO LOVE 'THE GRIND'?

As Marcia said, there's a difference between slog and grind. And sometimes you will get the two confused. Most of the time slog does in fact lead to grind, but if you're slogging away too much you may give up and never even get to 'the grind'. And that's not what we want, because then you'll never reach the success that lies on the other side.

So how do you know the difference between the right kind of discomfort and the wrong kind? And can you ever turn the wrong sort into the right sort? In other words, if you feel like you're slogging away, day in day out, what can you do to convert relentless, soul-sapping slog into motivating, uplifting grind?

First, let's think about the word 'slog'. Do you get a mental image of some poor bastard on their knees, a grimace on their face, looking as though they're about to give up on life? I know I do. Slog is hard. Slog is unrelenting. It can feel like you're giving everything and getting nowhere.

Surely you've had that feeling? I know I have. In my late twenties I took on a job on a big-name women's magazine. I thought it was my dream job. I was so excited. Of course, it was hard to start with. And that's okay because all new jobs should be hard, otherwise you're not pushing yourself. But the difficulty never seemed to abate. In fact, as time went on it only seemed to get harder and harder. I heard only the same criticism from my colleagues and, day after day, the excitement I had felt at the beginning started to drain away like water from a bath tub. I became anxious and angry, and then hopeless.

When I imagined my life in six months' time I just couldn't see any openings that would change my situation. In the end I resigned and went to work on a competitor title. That was hard too, don't get me wrong, but on this magazine the slog started to switch into grind quite quickly. I could feel progress and was promoted within the year. It never stopped feeling difficult, by the way, but it was a different kind of difficulty. It motivated me rather than crushing my spirit. It felt challenging rather than impossible. Every day felt like going into battle, except I was the hero at the front who could make all the difference, rather than the foot soldier at the back.

Do I feel resentment towards that earlier job? Absolutely not.

If I could manipulate time and erase it from my CV, would I? No way! It was absolutely crucial in helping me understand what negative slog looks like compared to positive grind. And that's how you should always chalk up a bad experience – whether it's a dead-end relationship, a tough job or a friendship that has hit the skids. They are essential to your understanding of the world and where your time and energy should ultimately be directed. When well-meaning people say, 'Just take my word for it', I think it's a crazy thing to say. Because what may be a hard slog for someone may not be for someone else. And besides, I'm a firm believer that you have to live through discomfort in order to not only test your own limits and capabilities, but also to understand what makes you tick.

Perhaps the easiest way for you to understand what a negative slog looks like is to compare it to a positive grind. This may not be the same for everyone, so it is just a rough guide. You will probably notice a few things that resonate with you.

Slog

- You feel like you're doing the same thing over and over again
- You find yourself *thinking* the same things over and over again
- You keep hearing the same feedback from those around you
- You feel less energised as time goes on
- You start to feel anxious, frustrated or even angry as time progresses
- You often can't remember what you have done that day

- You feel no sense of purpose
- You feel jealous when you hear people talk about feeling 'fulfilled'
- You cannot imagine anything ever changing

Grind

- You feel like you are making small incremental progress
- You feel yourself thinking about new ideas or new ways to attack what you're doing
- You hear encouraging feedback from those around you
- As time progresses you also hear different feedback from those around you
- You feel challenged but more energised as time progresses
- You start to feel uplifted, more determined and more engaged as time moves on
- You are hyperaware of everything you have done that day
- You feel invested and fulfilled in what you are doing
- You can imagine what success looks like on the other side

As you can see, while slogging it out may look like the same thing from the outside, it can feel very different when you're inside it. Marcia describes a negative slog to me like this: 'It's when you think you've got everything right – great idea, great business plan – and no matter how much you work, it just never seems to get any friction.'

Most of us would say: 'Well, it's not getting any friction because I've just not met the right people to invest in it yet.' Or I have heard people say: 'It's not working yet because people just don't understand the idea properly.' But here's the thing: if you are getting the same signs and signals from the outside world again and again and you are working at full capacity, slogging away day after day, and you think you can't improve on the idea, you need to ask yourself: am I in a negative slog or a positive grind?

That can be a tough question to ask because you've probably done a lot of work on your project. You may have invested money. You will almost certainly have invested time. But there has to come a moment when you ask yourself: can anything further change that is within my control? If the only thing that will change your situation is meeting an investor who really 'gets' it, then it may be time for a rethink. Because that person may never come along. You could end up slaving away for years and years, wasting time and, most crucially, your energy and optimism, on the small chance that fate may throw you someone with pots of money who likes your invention for a 'cold water bottle' (as in the opposite of a hot water bottle and, yes, I know someone who spent a long time trying to flog this idea). I'd say that's not a good enough life plan for you. Remember, you can only really go through good discomfort if you feel in control. Take the control away and be at the whim of an outside factor and it becomes a lot scarier. If you are in that situation, and have decided you're in a negative slog and it's probably time to pull the plug, then I've some good news: you haven't completely wasted your time.

Let me share with you a story of a young woman. For the

sake of this book and to mask her identity let's call her Madison (because, she tells me, she is shy rather than embarrassed and has always wanted to be called Madison). Anyway, about ten years ago she quit her job as an air stewardess to launch an app. It was a massage delivery app. Imagine Deliveroo, but instead of bringing Nandos and hot sauce to your door it delivered masseurs. She canvassed for a bit of feedback among her friends, who weren't so sure.

This was way before we were hailing taxis and jumping into strangers' cars through a small app called Uber. Besides, you were inviting strangers into your home *and* getting undressed. It just didn't seem *right*. (Now, of course, such an app exists called Urban Massage.) She did round after round of seeking funding and no one was interested. She also found it a struggle to get masseurs to sign up. They weren't sure about going into the homes of strangers and then asking for payment once the massage was over. (Yes, there was no direct debit method of payment – or PayPal transactional methods. Like I said, it was a while ago.)

Every time I saw her she would tell me the same thing: it was hard. No one would sign up. She was sick of making phone calls that always resulted in a no. And I mean it was like this *every* single time I asked her. Nothing in her situation ever changed, even though she was working flat out. Her morale started to dip. She became depressed, unable to see an end to the relentless slog. The only solution she could think of was to find an investor with 'true vision' she used to say. But the problem was she had tried most of the investors with a certified track record of 'true vision' – and not one of them wanted in. In the end, three years later, she threw in the towel.

Today she runs a very successful cleaning company delivering cleaners to your front door when and as you need them. It's not easy – there are lots of complaints and she must rely on her cleaning team to turn up, and on time, and work to a certain standard on every single job. But she feels energised. Every day is a challenge, but a 'good challenge' she tells me. She has a clear idea of what the next stage of the business is going to look like too and the noises from investors, friends and her peers is that she has stumbled upon a really great idea. Except she didn't stumble upon it at all.

'Part of the success of my new business is the learning from all that hard work I did on the massage app. I wasn't moving anywhere with that, but what I was doing, unbeknownst to me, was building a really strong template of what signs to look for the next time I started something, so that I wouldn't ever end up in that place again. Everything I did that didn't work the first time around I looked very closely at the second time around. It made me much more focused and meant I never saw any of that time as truly wasted.'

TURNING POSITIVE SLOG INTO GRIND

Cheffing can be an unremitting slog. Long hours, repetitive tasks, harsh taskmasters chivvying you along day in, day out. Ask any chef at the top of their game what it was like at the beginning of their career and they will say it was deeply uncomfortable. Often they worked long days, stood on their feet for hours at a time, barely ever saw sunlight and were given the very worst jobs in the kitchen.

I know of one female chef (let's call her Alice) who started her career in one of the best restaurants in the world. She was eighteen years old and for the first six months her entire job was to cut tiny, perfect squares of basil leaves to place atop an ice-cream dish. The squares would be inspected every day by the pastry chef and if they were even slightly bruised, or even one of the squares was not the right size, then he had her do the whole lot all over again. (The irony was that the squares were barely ever noticed by the diners, who removed them from their ice-creams almost immediately.)

And yet, she says it was one of the best experiences of her career, because she could feel the incremental changes taking place. Every day her mission was to get one less telling-off by the pastry chef. Every evening her plan was to have fewer and fewer bruised squares in the bin. It was tiny, uncomfortable change, but it was enough to make her feel her career was in forward motion. It was the same for many other chefs, who often speak fondly about their time starting out in the kitchen.

The cheffing structure is very hierarchal: you start as a prep chef doing things like cutting pieces of basil into squares, then move up to become a 'station chef' learning how to run a fish grill or make the perfect steak. Done that? Then you're on to becoming a sous chef, then an executive chef and so forth. The point is that, at every step of the journey, the discomfort of doing the job is tempered by the progress each individual feels they are making. That is good discomfort.

As Marcus Wareing, one of the world's most successful three-star Michelin chefs has said in the past: 'The key to succeeding as a chef is hard work and sacrifice. If you're clever you'll say you want to start at the bottom and work your way up.'

Alice did just this: 'I knew I was making progress with the basil leaves when I started to get a nod from my pastry chef rather than a snarl when he looked at my work. In time that nod turned into a pat on the back and that pat on the back then turned into me being promoted.'

So you see, positive grind is accompanied by small, subtle signs of progress. It may be something as small as an encouraging handshake or a 'well done'. In order for it to be positive you should notice a change. You should feel you are getting better and moving forwards, and the signals from the world around you should reflect that. If that's happening then you will feel energised, excited and motivated in exactly the same way that young prep chefs feel when they charge into work for an evening's service.

Tom Kitchin, also a Michelin-starred chef and one of the UK's most famous names, puts it perfectly: 'You need that extra energy and buzz when you're busy, day in day out, week in week out. The worst thing to happen in the restaurant – I'm sure most chefs will agree – is when you come to the next week and it's just that little bit quieter. That's when you've always got problems. People relax. The mentality, the edge disappears.'

10

EMPLOYING YOUR HUSTLE MUSCLE

Nix the discomfort of networking

A few years back I was writing a feature about couples who trained together, so I tweeted: *Looking for couples who work out together for a story. If that's you, contact me.* Within minutes a message appeared in my inbox. 'Hi Farrah. My name is Joe and I work out with my girlfriend. Happy to speak whenever.'

I phoned him. He had a slightly high-pitched voice, not unlike David Beckham's, and spoke with the sort of warm enthusiasm journalists are rarely met with. He was a personal trainer, he told me, and held fitness boot camps in the South London park near where he lived. He was also having some success with a body plan he had devised for his clients. We chatted for twenty minutes. I liked him. He gave proper, well-thought-through answers to every question I launched at him.

At the end of the conversation he told me that if I ever

needed any exercise or nutrition plans for other features then just to let him know and he could whip them up quickly for me. As it happened I *did* need someone to give me exercise tips for another story I was working on. Brilliant, I remember thinking. This will save me a huge amount of time. I asked him to send some ideas over. They arrived within the hour, perfectly written and exactly what I was looking for. What's more, at the bottom of the email he had written that if I ever wanted to try the body plan myself then just to give him a shout.

'What a nice, helpful guy,' I remember thinking. 'I'll use him again.'

By the time I did think of him again, however, it was too late. Eighteen months later he was a big star with the best-selling book of 2017. Profiles of him started to appear in the national press. He had a TV show and was worth hundreds of thousands of pounds from his body plans alone. The polite young man I had spoken to all those months ago was called Joe Wicks. Today he is arguably the most successful fitness star in the world. He is also the consummate hustler.

HONING YOUR HUSTLE TRADE-OFF

Let's just throw it out there for a minute: hustling is hard. No one enjoys doing it. It is plain and simple discomfort. There is the internal discomfort of what you think others will think of you while you do it. There is the practical discomfort of finding the right person to hustle in the first place. And then there is the literal discomfort of *asking* for something from someone to whom you have little to give in return.

When I was growing up, the term 'hustler' had bad con-
notations. Hustlers were basically crooks. Crooks or pimps.
If you hustled somebody, you were basically strong-arming
them into something they probably didn't want to do. I
remember overhearing my mum call one of our family friends
a 'hustler' once. I never thought of him in the same way again.
And for most of my adult life 'hustling' carried no badge of
honour. With its whiff of pushiness at best, and its whisper of
criminality at worst, it was most definitely an insult. But in
the last few years the term has had something of a renaissance.
Across social media people now actively boast about being
'on the hustle' or proselytise on how 'you've got to hustle
to get ahead'. You can buy T-shirts that say: 'Stay humble,
keep hustlin', and notebooks whose front covers declare: 'I'm
a hustler', as though it's the most aspirational thing in the
world. Someone called me a 'hustler' recently. She told me it
was a compliment.

Like most things today, you can blame Silicon Valley, where
'hustling' is all part of the self-starting game. Silicon Valley
worships at the altar of brave entrepreneurship. After all, part
of being a stand-out entrepreneur is being prepared to hustle.
You have to make opportunities for yourself. You have to put
yourself onto everyone's radar. When you're an entrepreneur
there is no company pension plan for security and no steady
income to fall back on at the end of the month. You've got to
sharpen your wits, hone your 'opportunity intuition' and be
ready to force yourself into every conversation where you and
your business deserve to be heard.

One of Silicon Valley's icons, Steve Jobs, was probably the
most famous hustler of all time, a man who, while in eighth

grade, wanted to build his own frequency counter. At the time, Hewlett-Packard was the biggest computer company in the world, so, figured twelve-year-old Jobs, he'd call them right up and see if they had any spare parts lying around.

He found their number in the Palo Alto phone book and made the call. As luck would have it, Bill Hewlett, the CEO answered. And guess what? Not only did he have some spare parts that he was willing to give to Jobs, but he also offered him an internship assembling frequency counters over the summer holidays. The hustle had worked *spectacularly*.

Jobs' philosophy around hustling was that you just had to ask and you would get: 'The secret is to make the call,' he said. 'Most people never ask, and sometimes that's what separates the people that do things from the people that just dream about them ... I've never found anyone who didn't want to help me if I asked them for help.'

He makes it sound so easy! So uncomplicated! Simply ask anyone to do you a favour and *voilà*, it will be done. His mantra has led to hundreds of thousands of people cold-calling companies asking for internships and jobs. It has led to people being bombarded at social functions by hustling entre-preneurs, cards in hand, asking for follow-up coffees and to 'schedule meet-ups' to discuss their business. My own social feeds are full of hustling young men and women eager to meet so they can 'pick my brain' or 'collaborate' on ideas together.

But what Jobs failed to mention was this: in order to hustle *successfully* you have to ask *and* have something to offer. True, long-term hustle that you can turn to time and again is not simply about putting your hand out in front of the right people. It's about asking with one hand and offering with the other. Yes, someone may help you if you ask once. Maybe even if you ask twice. But a third time and people's generosity has a tendency to wear thin. If you're sitting there thinking: 'You're wrong. I've had lots of people help me time and time again and I've given nothing in return,' then you're either:

A: very lucky. It appears you have stumbled upon the only group of people in human history who are willing to help you unconditionally however many times you want without any reciprocity. Congratulations! You probably don't need to be reading this book in that case. You have got a team of guardian angels who can do far more for you than any self-help book ever could. Permission to close this book *now*.

B: naïve. Maybe your benefactors haven't asked for anything in return, but think about your relationship to them. Do you have skills they may, at some point, need to turn to? Could their business in some way benefit from whatever it is you are hawking? Seriously, think long and hard about this one. I guarantee there is some potential crossover. Make no mistake, they will pull on those 'firmly attached strings' when they need to.

C: blinkered. You're not going to like this one I'm afraid, but turns out you're completely oblivious to the fact your contacts are getting pretty sick of the constant one-sided hustle. Sure, their help may still be there, but I guarantee that the more you ask, the less forthcoming they will become. Do they take longer to reply to your pleas? Do you hear from them far less often than you used to? If the answer is 'yes', then, you know that thing they have called patience? It's probably pretty threadbare right about now.

*

So, how do you hustle the right way? How do you hustle so effectively that you not only don't get backs up, but you actually charm your 'hustling target'? And how, most crucially of all, do you 'hustle' so that it doesn't feel so uncomfortable. People like Steve Jobs? Hustling was second nature to him, as was strolling around on a stage in front of the world as if he was in a supermarket. But for most of us, it's hard. *Really* hard. You feel awkward. And transparent. And you are acutely aware of how little the person you are hustling actually wants to be hustled. It doesn't do good things to a person's confidence. But what if I told you that there is an almost painless way to use your hustle muscle. A way that, the more you use it, the better, easier and stronger it becomes.

WHAT PANTS AND THE GREEKS CAN TEACH YOU ABOUT THE DISCOMFORT OF HUSTLE

Sara Blakely is the world's first female billionaire. You may not know her name, but you'll almost certainly know her business. She's the woman women can thank for being able to climb into a bodycon dress just a few days after Christmas, due to her miraculous knickers that can vacuum pack paunchy stomachs and undulating hips into even the teeniest outfits. Spanx seem a no-brainer to most of us, the sort of invention the entire *Dragon's Den* crew would sacrifice their own family to invest in. But it wasn't that way in the beginning. No one, and I mean *no one* was interested in a pair of pants that basically looked and felt like hosiery with the legs cut off. The only way Sara Blakely was able to get her $1 billion invention off the ground was through the discomfort of flexing her hustle muscle. Over and over again.

Take, for instance, the way she got her first order with US retailer Neiman Marcus. After weeks and weeks of relentless calls to try and secure a meeting with the buying director, Blakely finally got in front of her. She noticed, however, that she was losing the woman's attention midway through her pitch. So what did she do? She asked the buyer to accompany her to the toilet – a bold and no doubt uncomfortable move to make at the time. Once there, Sara pointed at her body without the support wear, then disappeared into the toilet and reappeared wearing Spanx. The woman was bowled over by the difference and placed an order for all seven Neiman Marcus stores across the country.

Sara Blakely's change of tack was genius. She recognised, in that crucial moment, that simply telling someone how brilliant her business was, was not enough. She had to prove to the buying director that her product was so miraculous that it would change the fortune of Neiman Marcus's hosiery department. In that moment, when she saw the woman's interest fading (probably because she had seen half a dozen pitches just like it that day), she realised she had to quickly make the hustle less about flogging her own product and more about how her business could help Neiman Marcus.

When Spanx was eventually stocked in Neiman Marcus, Blakely had to hustle once more. Knowing the store would only place another order if stock sold quickly, she contacted friends – some new, some old – who lived in those cities across

America where Spanx were being sold. She asked each one of them to go into a Neiman Marcus store, feign interest in the product and then buy a pair. As well as hustling everyone into believing that they were going to be part of one of the most revolutionary brand stories in history, she also mailed each and every one of those friends a cheque to cover their costs *and* they got to keep the product. That's a small point, but it's a crucial one. And here's why.

We think 'hustling' is simply about spotting an opportunity and then muscling our way in. But it's not. That is to misunderstand human nature. We are naturally tribal animals: thousands of years ago, back when we were wearing fur skirts and necklaces of woolly mammoth molars, to get ahead we had to get along with other tribes. That meant we relied on reciprocity: you give me something, I give you something. That means we're hardwired to expect something in return. (Of course, it wasn't like that within our own tribes: you gave without expectation, which goes some way to explaining why your family are about the only people you can ask something of without giving in return. To a point, of course.)

Crowdfunding, the seemingly miraculous phenomenon of social fundraising, understands this only too well. Sure, it's about giving money to a cause or a project that you believe in. And there's undoubtedly some hard selling thrown around by those who are hawking their goods. But the crowdfunding hawker also understands that part of their hustle is about what *you*, 'the hustled', get from investing in their venture.

A while ago *Cosmopolitan* interviewed some of the people

behind the most successful crowdfunded projects of the last few years. Almost all of them agreed that offering to *give* something in return for a donation was the best sweetener of all. (Interestingly 'status sweeteners', such as offering to publicly attach the donors' names to the project, worked best of all.)

So you see, Steve Jobs was wrong about hustling. He said all you had to do was ask and you would get. If you're Steve Jobs, that's easy. Everyone Steve Jobs asked was happy to help because he was Steve Jobs! Designers, technicians, journalists – everyone will help you if they think you ultimately have more to offer them than they do you.

But what if you're like the rest of us? What if you don't really have much that your target wants? That's a tough, uncomfortable call. Here's what you have to do: you have to figure out what it is that they want, then work out how *you* can help them get it. Or, if you're really smart, make them *believe* you can help them get it.

Bad hustle is saying: 'I want you to help me get what I want.'

Good hustle is saying: 'I've got something that is going to help you get what you want.'

The difference between the two is not only that one works more effectively than the other, but also that it will make you feel a hell of a lot less uncomfortable. Everyone wants to hustle with someone who has something they want. And like we said, hustling, by its very nature, is discomfort, so the idea is to ease that as much as possible while you're doing it.

A HUSTLE NO ONE CAN TURN DOWN

Joe Wicks saw his opportunity to hustle when I put that notice up on social media. He identified his hustle 'target' (the magazine I was working for at the time), but he also had the smarts to figure out that once he had made contact with his target, he needed to maximise the opportunity.

He did this in three ways. First, he gave me what I wanted. He knew I needed to talk to someone for a feature and he made himself readily available. But he also figured out that, as the editor of a fitness magazine, which I was at the time, I would probably also need expert exercise and nutrition plans at some point – after all, that was the bread and butter of *Women's Health*. (It's worth pointing out here that he also had *expert* knowledge of the magazine. I cannot tell you the number of people who have tried to hustle me without any knowledge of the magazine I work for, or even what I do. The number of strangers who email asking *Cosmopolitan* to cover them and their business while misspelling my name – Sara, Fara, Ms Store are all standard – and sometimes even putting the wrong magazine. This is bad hustle.) What's more, at the end of our dealings with one another Joe *then* offered me a chance to try out his body plan. He had used his hustle muscle so effectively that, by the end of the day I felt I was kind of hustling *him*.

Remember how I said Steve Jobs was wrong about hustling? That his advice to simply ask and you shall get was erroneous and basically misunderstood human nature? Well, while I still stand by that (given it was only six paragraphs ago that's probably a good job), but I also think Jobs underplayed just how skilled he was. For though he thought hustling was a case of asking for what you needed, he himself behaved in quite another way.

Let me give you an example. Back in the early 1990s the then twenty-six-year-old Jobs wanted to hire John Sculley to be CEO of Apple. Sculley wasn't convinced. He was CEO of Pepsi at the time, a company he had begun working for as a truck driver many years previously. He had loyalty to the brand. Loyalty and history. Jobs spent five months courting Sculley, having rejected twenty other candidates for the job. Finally, he offered it to Sculley, who said no.

Frustrated, and no doubt desperate to see opportunity slipping from his grasp, Jobs knew he had to flex his 'hustle muscle' even harder. So he dropped him the famous line that made Sculley reconsider. 'Do you want to sell sugar water for the rest of your life? Or do you want to come with me and change the world?'

In that moment, Jobs understood that simply hawking his job offer to Sculley wasn't enough. He had to figure out what Sculley *really* wanted. At this point Sculley had been a CEO for a few years. He'd also been earning a sizeable salary. Money and corporate power wasn't what interested him. But being remembered as the guy who helped lead one of the world's most pioneering companies? That was too seductive a hustle to turn down.

Jobs had a knack for doing this. He could convince anyone to do anything. But it wasn't because he asked. It was because he asked *and he offered* at the same time. He had a gifted intuition for knowing what the other person wanted. So much so that colleagues nicknamed it 'Steve's reality distortion field'. He represented reality not as it was, but as the other person wanted it to be.

HONING YOUR 'OPPORTUNITY INTUITION'

Before you even start to stretch your 'hustle muscle' you need to identify what it is you need, and who can best help you get it. Be realistic here too. While I'm a firm believer in aiming high, aiming for Gwyneth Paltrow to endorse your new wellness business is probably not going to happen – *yet*. The only thing you'll dent by shooting too high too early is your confidence. So think it through.

Make a list of around ten people. No more. Too high a number is going to be overwhelming and, besides, the beauty of successful hustling is that one connection invariably leads to another. What you don't want to end up with is so many contacts that you can't follow any of them up properly.

Now think about what it is you need from them. Is it advice? If so, what sort of advice? Be specific. The people that others most want to hustle are busy, so asking to have a vague coffee is not going to tempt them. Choose one thing you would like to discuss with them, two at a push. They will want to know that there is a limit to the help.

Next, research everything you can on them. Journalists do this as a matter of course before they interview anyone. We do this not because we want to talk to them about every aspect of their life, but because people can tell almost instantly when you have no knowledge of what they actually do. Don't ask me how, they just know. Today it's easy to find out information about anyone. Instagram accounts give you a window into the sort of person they might be and what they enjoy; Twitter can be an eye-opener on their views and what they read. And LinkedIn is a good, solid place to gain a sound understanding of their professional background and how their skills may cross over with what you need.

Once you've identified your 'hustling target', ask yourself: if they respond, can I get back to them quickly? Is my business plan ready for someone else to see? If they do agree to meet for coffee, do I have a very clear breakdown of what it is I want to talk about? Again, busy people tend to work in the moment. I've lost count of the number of people I've met in my career, who, when asked if I can meet them to follow up on an idea, choose to do it quickly. 'How about now?' is often their response. So ask yourself that question before you approach anyone. If they said to you: 'How about now?' would you be prepared? The answer should always be yes.

In a world of hustlers, speed, accuracy and aim is what counts. I cringe when I think of all the networking features I used to write for women's magazines advising people to hand their cards out to as many people as possible. Networking doesn't work like that. Certainly not today anyway. People can spot a hustling kamikaze a mile off. 'Working a room' is not what smart hustlers do. Working the one or two people that truly connect with you and what you do in that room? That's smart hustle.

KNOW YOUR VALUE

There's nothing more terrifying that walking into a room not knowing a soul and seeing the one person you want to hustle surrounded by a group of people. That requires stepping slap bang into your discomfort zone. The wobbly walk over, the way your mind frantically scans for an interesting opening gambit, the fear that you might have to stand there like an autograph hunter as you wait for your way in ... Gah! It's discomfort turned up to eleven. How do you soften *that*?

Well, you remind yourself of *your* value to *them*. The sheer psychological act of knowing you have something to offer them, rather than merely taking from them, makes it so much easier. Make a list of your top ten skills. What do you have that is unique to you? Maybe you're a brilliant writer. Perhaps you're a wizard with social media. It could simply be that you have lots of contacts in an area where the person you'd like to hustle has none.

Now look at them: what could you offer that would help them? Is there any crossover between what you do and they do? Can you spot any holes in their business that you could assist with?

Once you've done all of the groundwork then it's simply a matter of introducing yourself. Someone far wiser than me once told me it's always a good idea to shake someone's hand when you first meet them, look them in the eye and say your *entire* name. Chances are, they'll already know half a dozen people with the same first name as yours, so you want to stand out from the beginning.

Next, make your opening gambit a compliment. Tell them something you love about what they do. Not only will it show an awareness of them and their business, but it's psychologically a much easier way to make an initial interaction.

During the conversation ask them if there is anything you can help them with. Drop it into conversation. Something as simple as: 'In my last job I increased traffic to our website by 50 per cent in six months. I'm sure you don't need it, but if you ever need any assistance with that I'd be happy to help.' Even if they don't take you up on the offer they will recognise the generosity of it. And who doesn't want to be hustled by someone who is generous, complimentary and *appears* to be able to help you as much as you can help them?

CONCLUSION

The BMD method for life

Three years ago I decided to do a test. I wanted more out of life and, besides, I felt there was more of me to give. What if I had all these untapped strengths (and certainly unidentified weaknesses) that I had never been aware of before? How would I get to find out about them? How could I figure out if I was a decent public speaker, say, or if I could lead a large team unless I was pushed into doing it? I had just had my thirty-fifth birthday. Forty loomed large on the horizon. I wanted to see what I was made of.

Pushing yourself into your own discomfort zone is not easy. Often we only find ourselves there by chance, circumstance or by the force of someone else. Forcing yourself into a zone where things get harder, the pressure gets fiercer and you feel woefully out of your depth . . . few people can do that.

However, given that I knew from first-hand experience that I performed better when I worked outside my comfort zone, I had to figure out a way of placing myself there as often as possible. But I knew sheer strength of will alone would not do that. A lot of people (okay, *most* people) will take the path of least resistance given the option. Me included. There was only one answer: to start saying yes to things. Namely, lots of really scary things that would force me into my discomfort zone.

These were not things like jumping out of an aeroplane at 30,000 feet, by the way (I know my limits – that's one of them), but things I had always fantasised about doing but never quite had the fearlessness to go out and actually do. They were not personal goals but they *were* personal desires. Things that, if I was bold enough, I would do without a moment's hesitation.

The quickest way to shift them from mere desires into actual goals, I figured, was to agree to do them and then figure out later how I'd actually deliver. I said yes to a live political radio show even though politics has never been my thing. I said yes to hosting a dinner for thirty of the world's most senior women in tech, despite knowing pretty much nothing about the tech word. I said yes to speaking in front of an audience of 30,000 people and yes to a TEDx talk that would be broadcast around the world. I said yes to everything that a few years before I would have either declined or responded to with those five classic words: 'Can I think about it?' The problem with saying those words is that fear meanwhile gets hold of you, listing all the terrible things that might happen. Far better to say no and never have failed than to say yes and fail spectacularly.

This is why I developed something I call my 'personal mentor'. Bear with me here, because I know it sounds ridiculous – like the sort of thing someone would say while offering you a coconut husk of steaming ayahuasca and telling you to 'set your mind free'. But I'm serious.

I have had some brilliant mentors in my life, wonderful

women and men who have pushed me into my discomfort zone time and time again. I'm sure you have too. Over the years their belief in me has overridden my own lack of belief in myself. So much so that I have gone on to edit two magazines, something that I never thought I would be able to do. (I never, ever thought I would be an editor. I dared to dream it once or twice but always told myself that being a steady features writer on a newspaper supplement would be the limit of my ambition.) Mentors are a true gift that not everyone in their lifetime gets to experience. The only issue with them is that they cannot, nor should they, be relied upon to stick around. That's the beauty of them: they appear like little flickering lights along a long, dark road, guiding you towards your discomfort zone, then fading away so you can do the rest yourself.

Many of us find that we function better when we have a mentor. I know I always have. We do things we might not ordinarily have thought of doing before when we have our mentor pushing us from behind. Mentors don't take no for an answer because they see the enormous potential in us. They have a knack of knowing just how much we are capable of and exactly who we have the chance to become if we just apply a little self-belief. A mentor's guidance is a bit like stabilisers on a bike: essential in the beginning, but in no way required for you to keep moving forward.

But what if you don't have a mentor? What if you've never had someone to coax you along? What if you've never had a cheerleader, shouting and shimmying along the side lines, telling the world how exceptional you are? Then you become your own mentor.

Becoming a mentor to yourself might sound crazy, but, if

you decide to do it, you won't regret a single day, I promise. Because most of us know what the right direction of travel is for ourselves. We all know where we want to be and where we want to go. (And those of you who think you don't? That's because you've been too scared to let yourself even consider it. Sit back now and write it down. If there were no stresses and struggles in life, where would you want to be and what would you want to be doing? Hold on to that image. It will get you through everything.)

Having a personal mentor will release you from the fear of making the first bold step many of us need in order to do something new. Once you've taken the first step you can then use the BMD method to help you along the rest of the way. A personal mentor is going to change the way you think about yourself and the life you thought you were content to lead. It's going to open up the world to you – and, yes, that can be scary. But remember, fear is just excitement by another name.

The deal is simple: if you decide you are going to be your own personal mentor, then you need to listen to yourself. And you have to reward that voice too, even when you get something wrong. Oh, and you can't ever, *ever* ignore it. Which means you will end up saying yes to a lot of things you never would have agreed to before. Got that? Good, then we can move on and introduce you two.

MEETING YOUR PERSONAL MENTOR

So, who is your personal mentor? Well, you know that internal voice that speaks before anyone else? The one that gets supressed almost as soon as it's spoken up? That's your personal mentor. It's the voice that has a point of view when the boss asks a roomful of people if anyone has any thoughts on what they've just said – but that somehow gives way to the ballsy colleague who has a far less sophisticated take on things. It's the same voice that says 'yes!' when a colleague asks if anyone would like to present to the team, but fails to make itself heard and instead takes a silent backseat, *again*. It's the voice that says you *can* start your own business, work the hours you want and do something you truly love, but is quashed by a louder, more dominant voice that says: 'Don't be so bloody ridiculous. You'll end up impoverished, living under Lidl cardboard boxes for the rest of your life.' Management gurus call this bolshie voice of doom your 'inner critic'. I call it your 'ambition extinguisher' or, less decorously, bullshit that you should just ignore.

Like any good mentor your personal mentor should always be on the lookout for smart opportunities that work for you. And when it spots them? It should say yes. Immediately. Saying yes is such a simple act, but one that we suffuse with such pressure that we often duck away from it. In fact, some of us are so scared of saying yes that we subconsciously engineer it so that we don't even come near the opportunity in the first place. Sounds weird, right? But you will have done it, and I have done it, and millions of people across the world are doing it right now. Because it goes back to that old idiom: you can't fail at something you've never tried. But I say you can't open up your world unless you're willing to push down the door that allows you access in the first place.

Here's what's going to happen. You are going to say yes to something that you have always wanted to do. Every. Single. Month. It may not even be something you have always wanted to do, but if you know where your end goal is and, accepting that challenge is part of the route to getting you there, then you will say yes. Don't even think about it. Just nod your head, agree and then figure it out later. That's what I do. I find myself agreeing to all sorts of things without even thinking it through. As long as they are things that will set me on my path to becoming a better editor (which has always been my long-term goal) then I will do them. Because saying yes is the scary part. That's why you need to say yes instantly. Once it's done you can relax and start thinking about how you're going to be amazing at whatever it is you have just signed up for. And that's where the BMD method comes in . . .

THE BMD METHOD: A REFRESHER

You know when you need to yank a plaster off, but you're too scared to because you know it's going to hurt? Well the *entire* act of ripping the plaster off doesn't hurt does it? That's just fear screwing with you. No, the only bit that *really* hurts is the bit in the middle where the skin and adhesive are in a bit of a 'not-coming-up-for-air' embrace. It's probably about 30 per cent of the entire process. Not that much at all, when you think of it like that.

And you've been on rollercoasters in your life, I'm assuming. So you know that the *entire* two-minute ride isn't scary. It's only those few seconds when you're edging up to the top of the corkscrew and you rest there, teetering over the edge, like an Olympic diver poised on the lip of a diving board. Okay, *that's* scary. But it's only about 10 per cent of the whole experience. The majority of the ride is actually pretty nice.

It's only those tiny brief moments of discomfort, or BMDs as I call them, that are causing all the trouble. They're the ones stopping us from taking on bold new challenges. They're the ones that cloud an *entire* experience, making us believe it is *all* difficult, *all* painful and *all* worth swerving if it means an easier life.

But nothing is *all* pain. Nothing is *all* fear. And nothing is ever worth swerving if you want to have a rich, full life. No, the key is to say yes to life's most daunting challenges, remind yourself that 85 per cent of anything is totally within your reach, and the remaining 15 per cent? You can blast through that with the BMD method.

THE BMD METHOD IN ACTION

You can get through most things in life if you break them down into three chunks. The human brain likes 'three'; it's a solid number. It's the smallest number with which you can create a pattern. It has a nice rhythm too. It's how stories have been communicated to us since we were knee-high (*The* Three *Little Pigs*, *Goldilocks and the* Three *Bears*, *The* Three *Billy Goats Gruff*). That means we feel comfortable with it. And comfort is what you need when discomfort is what you're about to charge through.

Here's what you do when you have a difficult situation on the horizon. You break it down into the three worst-case scenarios that could happen. I'm talking about the moments you are really dreading. The ones which you think could derail the entire experience. Write them down. Okay, so these are your BMDs. (Once you start breaking things down into fours and fives it can start to become overwhelming, the pattern gets out of whack and your brain gets confused. Stick to three.) Got them? Okay, so now you need to start thinking about three solid solutions that can get you through these three BMDs. You probably won't use all three solutions but simply having them will make you feel at ease.

I'm going to give you an example. A few months into my role as editor of *Cosmopolitan* I was asked to interview a well-known female personality on stage in front of hundreds of people. I'm okay with public speaking now, but back then? No way. What made it worse was that my new colleagues were in the audience, as was my new boss *and* my CEO. Oh, and the person I was due to interview? Nightmare. Famous for being skittish, prone to saying outrageous things and not a fan of any personal questions. Only months earlier she had been involved in a public scandal, something I knew the audience would want to know about. If I didn't ask about it? Well, then I wouldn't have done my job.

When I agreed to the challenge I had said yes without thinking it through, but as the time approached I started to get nervous. I made lists and lists of questions that I tried desperately to memorise. The problem was, the more I tried to memorise them, the more I panicked about forgetting them. I was a mess. The nerves started to feel more like sickness. I got cramps whenever I thought about it. There was no way, I thought, that I could go through with it. It had become so monstrous, so all-consuming, that even I knew things had got out of control. This was bad discomfort in action.

So one evening, very late at night, I sat down with a pen and pad of paper and wrote out what I was scared about. When I was done I looked at the scrawl in front of me and noticed two distinct things. First, that I had written down only the absolute worst-case scenarios: getting the audience's attention when I first walked on stage; forgetting my questions; and asking the killer question about the public scandal. (See what I mean about the brain forming patterns of three?) The list, it turned out, was not long at all. Certainly not as long as I had imagined.

I started with the thing that terrified me the most. The one thing that was clouding everything: the walk-on. The walk-on is that moment when you walk on stage and have somehow to capture the attention of every single person in the room. It's hard. Really hard. In fact, it's plain hell on earth. (Ask any seasoned speaker and it's the thing they hate the most.) I thought to myself, what can I do that will mean I won't end up standing on stage pleading with a boisterous crowd to be quiet? It was especially important that I got this bit right too, because how I blasted through this BMD would set the tone for the rest of the interview.

I watched a ton of videos of people standing up to give speeches. And the more I watched, the more patterns I started to notice. They were these: everyone either began with a joke (way too high-risk for me); a question (doable, if it was the right question); an instruction or observation aimed at the audience (again, totally doable); or with the words 'I want to share with you a story . . .' (I guess we're hardwired to listen to anything that sounds like it's going to be juicy gossip).

Asking a question seemed to me to be the easiest option. Followed by an observation or instruction. And if that didn't work? Then I could fall back on telling them a story. Once I had my three-point plan, I felt instantly at ease.

My next 'discomfort point' was asking my interviewee a difficult 'personal' question. Okay, I reasoned, what was the best possible way to deal with this? I could do the cowardly thing and ask it near the beginning to get it out of the way, but then that would almost certainly set my interviewee on edge and, again, could derail the entire interview. I could do as many journalists do and leave it until the end, once they were feeling comfortable. But then, if the interviewee became hostile, I reasoned, the interview would end on a sour note and that would be all the audience would remember. Far better to plant it in the middle, after a gentle question, so they were feeling comfortable, and before a funny question so if it all went pear-shaped they could at least salvage the mood. So that's what I planned.

As for forgetting my questions. Pah! That was easy. Yes, I could try and memorise them (I still like to do this – it's a bad habit, so shoot me) but I also made sure I had a list of them in front of me, *plus* the ones I had trouble remembering the most I scrawled on the nook between my thumb and my forefinger. Turns out it's a comedians' trick – makes your hand look like the Rosetta Stone, but that's a small price to pay.

In the end the interview went brilliantly. I felt challenged, sure, but it felt exciting and invigorating, not frightening or overwhelming.

By the way, the BMD method works for *anything*. Frightened of reaching for the biscuit tin when you step through the front door after a hard day's work? Think of your three-point strategy. Mine? First: I don't change into my elasticated 'danger-pants' the minute I walk through the door – expandable waistlines incite expandable appetites, I find. Second: I moved the biscuit tin to the top shelf in my cupboard; that way it's just out of reach and I'm often too tired to find the willpower to reach for a step ladder to get up there. Three: I've swapped a cup of tea when I first get home for a cup of coffee. Coffee and biscuits don't taste quite the same as tea and biscuits. It's a simple, painless strategy.

STEP INTO YOUR DISCOMFORT ZONE

The BMD method works for anything. I know, because I have been doing it for the past five years, day in, day out. Not only has it changed the way I live my life, but how I see the world. One of my colleagues recently said she couldn't imagine me 'being scared of anything'. If only she knew that I used to be the woman who was scared and anxious about most things. And by the way, fear and anxiety are human emotions that worm their way into all of our lives. I wouldn't be human if I didn't experience them. But I take more risks now. I embrace challenge. Every time things get tough I remind myself that this is what it feels like when things are moving forward. This is what it feels like to charge through life.

Remember, stepping into your discomfort zone is not about eliminating fear. It's not about making the world a fearless place. But it is about making you more fearless. It is about understanding just how well equipped the human spirit is to push through obstacles, navigate tricky terrain and scale great heights. And once you know and understand this, *everything* changes. Doors magically open, not because someone has pulled them back for you, but because *you* have pushed them open. Opportunities begin to sprout like wildflowers, not because there are more of them out there, but because you are more open to pursuing them. And tough, heart-palpitating moments seem to drift away, not because the world is an easier place to live in, but because you are a smarter, tougher, stronger person than you were yesterday. That's what stepping into your discomfort zone gives you: real, true strength.

Once I discovered this I started doing all the things I'd once been too afraid of before. An example: despite being happily married, travelling alone is one of the things I have always craved. For me it is one of the most exciting things you can do – and the best way to get to know a city. I love travelling alone, I crave the solitude, but, apart from my mad dash to Paris when I was twenty-one, I didn't do it for many years. I was too scared of the small things, the brief moments of discomfort if you will – like eating out alone, navigating public transport in a foreign language and being a lone woman walking the city streets at dusk. But once I figured out the BMD method I no longer let those small niggles cloud the entire experience. Now, once a year, I go away to a foreign city by myself. It not only nourishes my soul, but, because I have been alone, I have met some incredible people who have, in turn, introduced me to other incredible individuals.

I'm no longer afraid of pitching up to work functions or dinner parties alone either. I simply identify where my BMDs will be – usually for me it's arriving and making the first introduction, that or getting stuck with someone and trying to make an immaculate escape without wounding their self-esteem. Recently, in fact, I was invited to a very grand home in central London where I didn't know a soul. The guests included a Baroness, several Silicon Valley wizards, a Harvard professor and . . . me. Several years earlier I would have either declined the invitation almost immediately (actually what I would have done is sat with it for a few days, so that fear had time to rake its icy fingers down my back – and then declined it) or accepted and then bailed at the last minute because of the sheer *perceived* discomfort of the whole thing. Not this time. I walked in there armed with a bottle of wine and a bunch of flowers (always take a few props, then you can at least ask someone to help you find a place for them, thus igniting conversation with someone so you don't look a complete lemon there by yourself) and made myself at home. It was a spectacular evening. I made more connections than I have in years, and several of those guests I now consider friends.

As for what this week brings? I have two dinner parties booked in where I don't know a soul, and one public debate with a very high-profile editor who, years ago, was actually *my* career crush. And I'm due to give an address at the House of Lords. These are all things I agreed to immediately. They are things I did not sit on for fear that fear itself would force me to decline the opportunity. I am in no way exceptional. I am an average journalist. I am an okay editor. I am not the world's best public speaker. But what I will do that most people won't is this: I step into my discomfort zone every single week. And what that has done is brought me opportunities that I never believed would come my way. As for

Cosmopolitan, when I stood in my glass office that warm June morning in 2015 I could see the discomfort that lay ahead. But it was the discomfort that allowed us, within just six months, to go back to being the country's number one young women's magazine – the first time this had happened in sixteen years.

All the brilliant women and men in this book were not born that way either. Victoria Pendleton, Sean Rad, Marcia Kilgore ... none of them would say they were any stronger or more gifted than you or I. But what they did have was the gift of being pushed, time and again (some by parents, others through circumstance) into their discomfort zones – just as my team are day in, day out. And because of that they know just how capable the human spirit is. They know that 'problems' are just a state of mind rather than a state of being and that challenge is what lifts us up, not pulls us down. They know that the only true way of testing the perimeters of human potential is by stepping into their discomfort zones. They understand the magical and, frankly, mysterious things that happen to both body and mind when they enter this realm. Just as you will too, once you take the first step.

ACKNOWLEDGEMENTS

There are so many people who have inspired this book – tough women and men who have taught me about the power of embracing discomfort. In no order whatsoever a big thank-you to: Anna Jones (for believing in me from the beginning), WD Storr (for all the helpful brainstorming on our dog walks), Rosette Pambakian, Rebecca Ridge and all my wonderful team at *Cosmopolitan*, who are put through their discomfort paces every single day. I'd also like to thank Emily Murphy and Jessica Browning.

Also a tremendous shout-out to my brilliant agent Adrian Sington, my wonderful editors Zoe Bohm and Anna Steadman, the mighty Clara Diaz, Aimee Kitson, Jillian Stewart and Alison Sturgeon.

And, of course, thank you to all my incredible interviewees who gave their time (and their secrets about how they embrace discomfort): Marcia Kilgore, Sean Rad, Victoria Pendleton, Sadja Mughal, Sabrina Cohen-Hatton, Eric Underwood and Tasha Eurich.

INDEX